To my children, Nancy and Jim

The HIKE IT SKI IT RIDE IT PADDLE IT BIKE IT WALK IT DISCOVER IT TASTE IT EXPLORE IT DRIVE IT GUIDE

to Ottawa, the Gatineau, Kingston and Beyond

Ann Campbell

The BOSTON MILLS PRESS

Copyright © 2001 Ann Campbell

Published in 2001 by
Boston Mills Press
132 Main Street, Erin, Ontario N0B 1T0
Tel: 519-833-2407   Fax: 519-833-2195
e-mail: books@bostonmillspress.com
www.bostonmillspress.com

An affiliate of
Stoddart Publishing Co. Limited
895 Don Mills Road, Suite 400, 2 Park Centre
Tel: 416-445-3333   Fax: 416-445-5991
e-mail: gdsinc@genpub.com

Distributed in Canada by
General Distribution Services Limited
325 Humber College Boulevard
Toronto, Canada M9W 7C3
Orders: 1-800-387-0141 (Ontario & Quebec)
Orders: 1-800-387-0172 (NW Ontario &
other provinces)
e-mail: cservice@genpub.com

Distributed in the United States by
General Distribution Services Inc.
PMB 128, 4500 Witmer Industrial Estates
Niagara Falls, New York 14305-1386
Toll-free: 1-800-805-1083
Toll-free fax: 1-800-481-6207
e-mail: gdsinc@genpub.com
www.genpub.com

05 04 03 02 01   1 2 3 4 5

THE CANADA COUNCIL   LE CONSEIL DES ARTS
FOR THE ARTS   DU CANADA
SINCE 1957   DEPUIS 1957

*We acknowledge the Canada Council, the Ontario Arts
Council, and the Government of Canada through the
Book Publishing Industry Development Program (BPIDP)
for their financial support of our publishing program.*

Canadian Cataloguing in Publication Data

Campbell, Ann, 1942–
The hike it bike it walk it drive it guide to
Ottawa, the Gatineau, Kingston and beyond

Includes index.
ISBN 1-55046-337-3

1. Outdoor recreation – Ontario,
Eastern – Guidebooks.
2. Ontario, Eastern – Guidebooks.
3. Outdoor recreation – Quebec (Province) –
Outaouais Region – Guidebooks.
4. Outaouais Region (Quebec) – Guidebooks.
I. Title.

FC3057.S73 2001   917.13'7044
C2001-930307-6   F1057.7.S73 2001

Printed in Canada

Design by Chris McCorkindale and Sue Breen
McCorkindale Advertising & Design

Photography by Ann Campbell and Nancy Steeves

The information in this guide is true and
complete to the best of my knowledge. If errors
are found or if there are favourite places of
yours that were left out, please provide details
in care of the publisher.

Cover (left): Ottawa's Winterlude

Cover (right): Hikers rest along the
Trans Canada Trail

Page 1: Champlain Lookout

CONTENTS

PREFACE

O n January 22, 1994, I stepped from Calgary–Ottawa Flight 905 and sensed deep in my heart that I had "come home." I also knew that an exciting career opportunity, new acquaintances, and the whole of Eastern Ontario and Western Quebec awaited my discovery. My expectations on all fronts have been exceeded five fold.

It was one cold, crisp, mid-February evening that my outdoor explorations began. Together with my newest friend, I marvelled at Winterlude's crystal masterpieces and watched skaters glide along the Rideau Canal under the moonlight.

Since then, I've cycled on one of the most picturesque and historic paths in Canada, hiked to see a mysterious field of boulders, attended wonderful concerts under the stars, and encountered thousands of Canada geese stopping to rest before heading south. I have photographed romantic covered bridges, found wonderful places to take the kids, and have savoured the bounty of summer at scenic picnic spots. I even know where you can sneak indoors to buy a little something from the sixth food group when no one is watching.

My children will tell you I'm not always good at keeping secrets, so I invite you to come along with me now and I'll tell you about some of the wonders I have uncovered in my extended backyard. I promise to take you to great places, so that you too may experience the beauty and tranquility, or the excitement and fun that fill the outdoors and my life in this part of Canada.

ACKNOWLEDGMENTS

Writing this book has been great fun. I could not have done it, however, without the never-ending help, encouragement and love of my children, family, friends, CIHI colleagues and fellow Context graduates. As well, I am most grateful to the many, many outdoor enthusiasts and tourism specialists throughout Eastern Ontario and Western Quebec who have always willingly assisted me with my research, travels, and editing. Extra-special appreciation goes to my daughter Nancy, and to the many staff of the National Capital Commission who know so much about this wonderful part of Canada.

Whatever their contribution towards making my dream come true...I thank them all!

INTRODUCTION

Outdoor, according to my well-worn Webster's dictionary, means "done in, located in, or suitable for the open air." In my mind, being outdoors can mean hiking to Pink Lake to revel at its fragile beauty, or swishing down a Laurentian slope. It also encompasses grooving to rock 'n' roll under the moon and stars on the shore of the St. Lawrence, attending a 188-year-old country fair, exploring the historic locks of the Rideau Canal, and snapping photos of the Governor General's Foot Guards on Parliament Hill. It means having fun and creating memories.

Although I reside in central Ottawa, for the purposes of this book's explorations the outdoors is considered to be those places in Eastern Ontario and Western Quebec that can be reached within a few of hours of my home. Most outings mean a day away. Some, however, beg me to stay a bit longer, to soak up more of the ambiance of the particular locale. I hope this happens to you!

The average person can undertake all explorations if they're in reasonable shape and ready for a little action. They're meant for those who want to enjoy the outdoors at a leisurely pace, rather than at 100 kilometres per hour.

I have divided the book into five sections: "Sightseeing on a Bicycle," "Exploring on Foot," "Excursions by Car," "Outdoor Spectacles," and "Discovering More Outdoors." Each of these starts with a short introduction. Thereafter, the first three include write-ups that will take you on specific step-by-step adventures.

In the last two sections, the approach is entirely different. Rather than looking in detail at one particular event or activity, each sub-section contains information about several places that will provide a unique kind of experience. For example, when music festivals are discussed, details on a number of popular events are provided.

To get full benefit from this book, three things are important. First and foremost, keep it accessible, so you can plan a variety of outdoor getaways often. Second, take it with you to find your way and to learn more about things to see and do once you're there. And last but not least, there is a page at the end of the book for notes, so before you leave make use of it to jot down last-minute details. Along the way, record highlights elsewhere as well that will serve as reminders when you sit down later to record your memories in a diary or photo album.

Useful Contacts

Every effort has been made to make the information provided for each outing both accurate and comprehensive. On the other hand, because one of the only constants in today's world is change, exact dates, hours of operation and site or activity costs are excluded. As much as possible, I've mentioned the general time frame when an event occurs, and if I'm certain there's a charge of some sort, I've added a ($).

To assist you in finalizing things before you set out, in most instances phone numbers and website addresses are listed. As well, the central contact numbers below may prove helpful. Please note: if an area code is not listed it's always 613.

Capital InfoCentre: 239-5000 or 1-800-465-1867 www.capcan.ca	**Outaouais Tourist Association:** 819-778-2222 or 1-800-265-7822 www.tourisme-outaouais.org
Ottawa Valley Tourist Association: 732-4364 or 1-800-757-6580 www.ottawavalley.org	**Gatineau Park:** 819-827-2020 or 1-800-465-1867 www.capcan.ca
Ontario East Tourism Corporation: 1-800-567-3278 www.ontarioeast.com	**Laurentians Tourisme Quebec:** 450-436-8532 or 1-800-561-6673 www.laurentides.com

Things to Bring Along

No matter which outdoor activity you're up to, check this list of not-to-be-forgotten items before leaving.

- personal identification including emergency contacts
- driver's licence
- medic-alert bracelet or necklace
- important phone numbers, change and a phone card
- admission fees, extra cash and a credit card
- comprehensive Ottawa city, and Ontario or Quebec highway maps
- Gatineau Park or Ottawa Greenbelt maps
- notebook and pen
- sunscreen, sun hat and sunglasses

- water, water, water!
- picnic or snack
- camera
- binoculars
- medications and first-aid supplies
- insect repellent
- clothing suitable for the outing, including rain gear and extra layers
- outdoor sports equipment with a lock
- plastic bags
- a sense of adventure and fun

Whatever you do, don't leave valuables in your car or its trunk, as we all know there are some in this world that can't resist temptation. To remove this opportunity, leave extra credit cards, cash and expensive electronic gadgets at home or in the hotel safe.

If you need to rent some outdoor equipment, give these outlets a try, or check the phone book's yellow pages.

Ottawa:		
• Cyco's	bicycles, in-line and ice skates, cross-country skis	567-8180
• Rentabike	bikes, in-line skates	241-4140
• Trailhead	tents, canoes, kayaks	722-4229
• Expedition Shop	snowshoes, tents	241-8397
• Mountain Equipment Co-op	canoes, kayaks, cross-country skis, snowshoes	729-2700
Hull:		
• Cycle Bertrand	tandem bicycles	819-772-2919
• Gatineau Park	snowshoes, canoes, kayaks, mountain bikes	819-827-2020
• Greg Christie's	mountain bikes, cross-country skis	819-827-5340
• Gerry and Isabel's	cross-country skis, snowshoes	819-827-4341
Cornwall:		
• Bicycle World	bicycles	932-2750
Kingston:		
• Ahoy Rentals	bikes, water sports equipment	539-3202

Getting There

As directions for outings in the first three sections of the book begin from central Ottawa or Hull, notes are included under the "Start" heading of each one to direct you to the launch point. Just in case you don't know the area or didn't bring along a map of downtown Ottawa (obtain one at a hotel or the Capital InfoCentre), I have prepared the table below to get you on your way at least as far as the four "Start" places are concerned.

In all four instances, travel east away from Parliament Hill on Wellington and Rideau Streets past the Château Laurier Hotel and then...

If The Text Titled "Start" Says	Find This Place
From Ottawa, take Highway 417	Continue on Rideau Street to the first corner after the Rideau Centre. Turn right here onto Nicholas Street and then travel ahead until it is time to choose the Highway 417 East or Highway 417 West exit ramp (Highway 417 is also known as the Queensway).
From Hull, take Highway 5 or Highway 148	Continue on Rideau Street and turn left onto Sussex Drive at the second traffic light after the hotel. Travel ahead and go right at King Edward and follow the signs to Hull over the Macdonald-Cartier Bridge to locate the directional signs for the highway of your choice.
From downtown Ottawa	Follow exactly the same directions as those to Hull above but this time turn much sooner to the left onto St. Patrick Street immediately after the National Peacekeeping Monument. There, directly across from the National Gallery of Canada beside Major's Hills Park, you will find yourself at the Ottawa end of the Alexandra Bridge (Interprovincial Bridge) at the Mackenzie Avenue intersection where a few outings begin.
From downtown Hull	Follow exactly the same directions as those to downtown Ottawa, and cross the Alexandra Bridge (Interprovincial Bridge) to arrive in Hull at the Laurier Street intersection, the starting point of some excursions.

Once you're in gear and at the "Start" spot, further notes are included within each write-up to complete the excursion. In case you decide to join an outing along the way or from another direction, you will need to rely on a good city or highway map, something I always carry in my car just in case.

The maps are also sure to come in handy when you're off to enjoy an "Outdoor Spectacles" or "Discovering More Outdoors" adventure as specific directions are not always included.

The Quebec Influence

Adventures throughout Quebec are particularly rewarding. The landscape is beautiful and the joie de vivre of the people is something that will be long remembered. When you travel in Quebec you may encounter someone who doesn't speak English. If you're an Anglophone, whatever you do, don't let this thought keep you away. Instead, communicating in charades of sorts or drawing a picture works most times.

Directions throughout the book use the English or French name depending on which seems more natural to me under the circumstances. Below, a few French words with their English translation are included to help you get the most out of your Quebec explorations.

French	English
nord	north
sud	south
est	east
ouest	west
plage	beach
lac	lake
ruisseau	creek or brook
rivière	river
montagne	mountain
belvédère	lookout
chemin	road
route	highway
rue	street
rue principale	main street
boulangerie	bakery
casse-croûte	snack bar
dépanneur	corner store
magasin général	general store
épicerie	grocery store
gîte du passant	bed and breakfast

One Last Thing

As I've said before, Mother Nature has provided me wonderful experiences in Eastern Ontario and Western Quebec. Over the years I have come to know her well.

What I like most is her open-door policy: If you treat my home with responsibility and respect, you are welcome anytime.

When I get a chance to visit, I always look around and notice the magical place she has created. Her choice of decor is impeccable—the colours, textures, lighting, music, perfumes and accessories are always perfectly arranged and never out of style. As well, I enjoy her houseguests. Believe me, they're quite the gang.

As you read further, I invite you to often give yourself the gift of a day in her home. I know they'll be times to remember.

Hikers at Meech Lake

Notes

SIGHTSEEING ON A BICYCLE

Have you ever thought about what you notice when cycling? Is it a mother bird leading her brood across the tranquil water, the interesting façade of a hidden mansion, or the caress of a warm summer breeze on your face amidst the silence of the forest?

Eastern Ontario and Western Quebec boast wonderful cycling routes, many of which should be stop-and-go affairs, because there are so many historical and beautiful sights to soak up along the way. Others should get your heart racing or slow your mind down. No matter which you choose, all provide adventure, a getaway, and a healthy form of exercise.

Most trips described in this section are on well-maintained recreational pathways, so a confident beginner can master them all. If you're pressed for time, tackle part of an excursion only. Do the same thing if it's a family outing, as young children are sure to tire before a circuit is completed. Along the way, check periodically on those calf muscles—sooner or later you have to pedal back.

A road or hybrid bike with three or more gears is all you need to get rolling. To rent one, check the "Things to Bring Along" page for rental ideas. Pack a bottle of frozen water and a lock, preferably one that's long enough to wrap around a tree or fence, just in case you have to improvise when looking for a place to secure your bike. If you're planning to cycle on an out-of-the-way route, consider bringing a repair kit.

As far as clothing goes, cycling shorts and gloves will cushion those tender spots, and a properly adjusted helmet is a must. It should be worn low on the forehead, just above your eyebrows, and shouldn't shift on your head no matter what. Buy a new one every few years before it dries out and develops cracks.

Cycling along the Ottawa River.

Safety should always be your number one concern. Remember that a bicycle is a vehicle, and when moving it is part of the traffic, be that cars, in-line skaters, joggers or lovers out for a stroll. Share the path, sound a bell or call out when passing and look ahead to see what's coming, rather than down at the ground. And use your gears to make cycling fun.

As it is impossible to read and pay attention to your cycling simultaneously, it is critical to review the details of an excursion in depth before setting out. Decide where you're going to stop—key interest points are highlighted in italics to assist in this regard—and then in many cases, it's simply a matter of following the yellow line or your nose to get there. It's best to have a frame-mounted bike bag to carry your stuff, and this book so you'll have it handy for quick reference. By the way, forget the backpack—it will alter your centre of gravity and may cause you pain now or down the road.

As far as the directions go, each excursion begins with a section that describes how to get to the starting point. Next, there are notes on the route itself, along with some handy tips about this and that.

Here and there, distances and completion times are also mentioned. The latter are based on cycling the whole route at a moderate pace and not stopping to visit any of the attractions along the way. It will be a real shame if you don't do this, so add some sightseeing time and make a day of it.

When you're sitting down to plan a cycling trip, here's one last thought: be innovative—don't rely solely on the excursions in this section for cycling ideas. Instead, study any of the "Excursion by Car" routes and make all or part of one a cycling adventure. For example, make a circle from Merrickville up to Burritt's Rapids and back. Cycle the back roads around Glen Tay in search of coloured leaves. Test your fitness level on the Gatineau Park parkways on a sunny "Sunday Bikeday." Whatever you do, get pedalling! You'll decrease stress, your weight and the risk of chronic disease, and increase your energy levels, fitness and family fun.

Parliament Hill Splendour

Start: Between mid May and mid October when the locks are operating, from downtown Ottawa, proceed on the marked bike path toward the Alexandra Bridge and go left at the driveway. Look for the Ottawa River Pathway sign. At other times, proceed along Mackenzie Avenue to the Château Laurier Hotel. Turn right and then left onto Elgin. Go left at the end of the National War Memorial and cycle down the driveway beside the National Arts Centre. Turn left and travel under the bridge and down the hill.

Route: Starts with a very steep incline and has a couple of mini hills later. Most of the route is off road and great for in-line skating.

Keep both hands firmly on the brakes as you begin your descent down, down, down the very steep, paved pathway to the Ottawa River, where you'll uncover an absolutely breathtaking vista.

If your timing is right, there'll be pleasure boats ascending or descending the eight *Ottawa Locks*. Before lifting your bike up onto the second lock gate, take a seat on the bench to the right to absorb the ambiance of this historic place. Just imagine how Lieutenant-Colonel John By and the Royal Engineers must have felt when the last tree was cut and the last slice of rock removed to make this 202-kilometre water highway from here to Kingston, at the head of Lake Ontario.

Look up to see the Canadian flag fluttering atop the *Peace Tower*, and *statues of Robert Baldwin and Sir Louis-Hippolyte Lafontaine*. The Province of Canada embraced the principles of responsible government that the two developed back before Confederation. To the left is the luxurious, castle-like *Château Laurier Hotel*. In 1912 Canada's first Francophone prime minister, Sir Wilfred Laurier, cut the ribbon to open this grand inn, which was built to accommodate politicians, ambassadors and well-to-do businessmen, many of whom arrived in Canada's capital via Union Station, formerly across the road.

> **Hints**
> It takes one hour to cycle this route of about 16 kilometres; add time to stop and start along the way to observe Canadian history from a new angle. For a longer outing, add a trip to Andrew Haydon Park once you reach the Champlain Bridge.

Cross over the lock and go right, onto the *Ottawa River Pathway* beneath the cliffs of Parliament Hill, and soon you'll notice the large stone *Ottawa Carbide Company Mill* on Victoria Island. Ottawa was once an important lumber town, so electricity generated using the Chaudière Falls upstream saw the first hydroelectric plant in the country and several mills constructed here in the late 1800s.

Detour right on the paved trail, shortly before the cycling pathway reaches a dead end, to locate the end of the 300-kilometre *Rideau Trail* that extends from here to Kingston on Lake Ontario. Someday, hike this route in its entirety to log yet another first in your outdoor-memory book.

Retrace your way to the pathway and follow the yellow line through the tunnel under the Portage Bridge. Take another side trip here up onto the bridge, and cross it part way on the Parliament Hill side to find where *Aboriginal Experiences* ($) provides another glimpse of Victoria Island's life hundreds of years ago. First Nation's people set up camp here when the Ottawa River was their major trading highway; today, a cultural event allows visitors a chance to tour a native village, sample traditional cuisine and take part in a friendship dance alongside native dancers in their colourful regalia. Call 564-9494 or 1-877-811-3233, or get more information at www.aboriginalexperiences.com.

The majority of locks are manually operated.

Back on the Ottawa River Pathway again, continue on and you'll find the *Trans Canada Trail Pavilion* displaying the names of the many who have donated towards building what will be a 16,800-kilometre shared trail. Actually, the cycling path between here and the Champlain Bridge is one small section of that vast network.

Cycle over *Pooley's Bridge*, past the Waterworks Plant, to see the LeBreton Flats Campground ($), a spot that provides a downtown-Ottawa tenting location for up to 300 persons from mid June to early September. For more information call 236-1251 in season.

Continue until you're back at the river and soon passing the gates to the Lemieux Island Water Filtration Plant. Watch for Jonathan Livingstone Seagull soaring higher and higher, as the rest of the flock screeches their welcome at *Lazy Bay*, with its mini version of the Thousand Islands. Stop to enjoy the mighty river's wide-open panorama, including the Little Chaudière Rapids in the distance.

Just before the Remic Rapids Lookout, watch for impressive *limestone sculptures* dotting the shallow water. For years, Jon Ceprano arranged the rocks to depict themes such as a wedding arch, fertility and integration. These stone masterpieces brought him international recognition. Stop for photos and a chance to construct a small creation of your own on the shore.

Further along, you can soon tell that Canada geese and other waterfowl love this tranquil stretch of water. Look for the fountain beside the Champlain Bridge parking lot for a chance to slurp a refreshing drink before using the sidewalk to cross the bridge from Ontario to Quebec. Halfway there, stop awhile at *Bate Island* on the right to watch the adventurous kayakers ride the raging Remic Rapids. Continue and turn right at the end of the bridge to head back to Ottawa, this time on the *Voyageurs Pathway*. At the river's edge, the old log makes a people-friendly place to reflect and picnic, as you observe the rapid's water dancing in the sunshine and a family of ducks sunning themselves on the rocks nearby.

The path now becomes a woodland delight on the way to the beach at *Mousette Park* (with washrooms and a concession). Later, read about the statue in *Brébeuf Park* before getting ready to challenge some hills and a hairpin turn or two. Stay alert, as the leaves often block out the sun. As well, because the path's surface is ultra smooth, in-line skaters, joggers, toddlers on training bikes, and couples out for a walk often share your space.

Soon, some of Ottawa's most historic sights come into view. In *Portageurs Park*, John McEwan's impressive sculpture, Boat Sight, is worth a stop. The vessel, seen here arriving on land, is said to represent culture, whereas the dog and wolf nearby depict nature responding to the event with fear and curiosity. Outside the park's gate, turn right, onto the sidewalk, and you'll be in the heart of *Hull*, an important part of Canada's capital region.

Proceed cautiously on the road with the vehicular traffic through the Chaudière Bridge intersection. Unfortunately, the famous Chaudière Falls are closed to the public. These natural impediments abruptly blocked the upstream progress of early explorers like Champlain, LaVérendrye and David Thompson, who were travelling the fast-moving river by birch-bark canoe.

But they didn't stop an influx of traders, missionaries and settlers from coming at least this far. By 1800, Philemon Wright, a United Empire Loyalist from Massachusetts, had arrived by horse-drawn sleigh along the frozen Ottawa. He settled on its north shore, and by spring recognized the value of the area's vast timber resources and the strategic importance of the churning Chaudière Falls to power mills that would convert these riches into lumber. Before long, log booms jammed the river, and machines began producing wooden beams and sheets of pine. Nearby, grain became meal and flour, and Wright's Town began to flourish.

About 50 years later, 24-year-old Vermont businessman Ezra Butler Eddy founded a wooden-match factory near the falls that would provide a source of employment for many more residents of Wright's Town. By day, the men toiled in the factory, while the women stayed home to make matchboxes and mind the children. Soon after Eddy set up shop, small-time carpenter John R. Booth moved from Quebec's Eastern Townships. Booth began manufacturing split shingles and windows and doors. His timing was perfect, as all facets of the lumber industry were the name of the game in these parts in the early nineteenth century. Imagine his good fortune when years later he was asked to supply the timber for the Parliament Buildings!

Progress didn't stop there. By 1875, Wright's Town had grown so much that it had become a city known as Hull. Today, some of its 65,000 mainly Francophone residents are among the civil servants who work in the federal government buildings along this cycling route.

Continue cycling through the Portage Bridge intersection, and go immediately right, up onto the Portage's southeast sidewalk to rejoin the Voyageurs Pathway again. You'll find a wonderful view of the building housing the *National Archives of Canada* and the *National Library of Canada* (the large concrete building with the black roof, closest to the bridge), the first historic spot to unfold across the river. Heritage manuscripts, government records, maps, prints, photographs, television programs, sound recordings and other parts of Canada's published heritage are preserved there. Many people visit to trace their Canadian ancestors, or to view Glenn Gould's favourite piano.

In the *Supreme Court Building* nearby, nine justices in traditional garb preside over Canada's highest court. The *Confederation Building*, with the green roof, houses government offices. Keep a sharp eye peeled for *Time Span*, a 9.7-kilogram, 3.5-metre fibreglass ball that keeps time as it moves along the curved roof atop the World Exchange Building.

Parliament Hill looks spectacular from here, with its majestic Peace Tower stealing the spotlight. As the centrepiece of both Canadian democracy and the City of Ottawa, the Centre Block houses the House of Commons, the Senate and offices for the cabinet and members of Parliament. Within this Gothic-style building, Canada's laws are debated and approved.

The magnificent circular, domed Parliamentary Library, seen behind the Centre Block, escaped the devastating fire the night of February 3, 1916, when flames ripped through Parliament Hill's Centre Block after a coal-oil lamp upset. What a miracle that a quick-thinking clerk slammed the heavy fire-proof doors. This saved the hundreds of carved-wood flowers, masks and mysterious creatures that make both the interior and exterior of this structure a Parliament Hill highlight. Tours are offered daily of the magnificent library and rebuilt Centre Block, except on New Years, Christmas and Canada Day.

On the left of the Voyageurs Pathway now is the *Canadian Museum of Civilization*. This fabulous building, designed by renowned native architect David Cardinal, symbolizes the moving glaciers, winds and other forces of nature that shaped our land. In the summer, voyageur canoes ($) leave the riverside park with paddlers wanting to experience how the fur traders and early settlers felt when they arrived here on the Ottawa River.

Inside the museum ($), magnificent totem poles and war canoes explain life in a Haida village, and a reconstructed archaeological dig shows the painstaking work involved in unearthing Canada's history. A special-exhibit area and the much-loved children's museum are on the second floor, while the top story provides an informative sight-and-sound journey through the past 1,000 years in Canada. For information call 776-7000 or 1-800-555-5621, or visit www.civilization.ca.

To reach the deck of the *Alexandra Bridge* from here, leave the museum's grounds and go under the bridge. Continue left up to the parking lot's entrance. Go left, cross at the traffic lights and then up onto the marked sidewalk bike path. Notice that the Ottawa Locks now look like a giant flight of stairs.

Watch for *Nepean Point* high up on your left as you soak up this postcard-perfect panorama. A statue of French explorer Samuel de Champlain stands proudly looking over the scene he came upon when he travelled up the Ottawa River in 1613—a scene featuring the rocky, rugged Canadian Shield to the north and rich, fertile lowlands further south. Completing the picture were many lakes and streams; stands of red, white and jack pines; sugar and red maple forests; and many species of plants and animals. The Astrolabe open-air theatre, named after the ancient navigational tool in Champlain's hand, was built on this site in 1967.

Next door, the *National Gallery of Canada* houses many of the nation's most-loved art treasures in its permanent collection, and travelling exhibitions from around the world ($) are also showcased here regularly. Call 990-1985, 1-800-319-2787, or go to www.nationalgallery.ca.

Major's Hill Park ends my favourite cycling trip. Established in 1874 as Ottawa's first park, the site recognizes where Colonel John By once lived with his wife Esther and two daughters in a two-story home with a wrap-around veranda and a fine flower and vegetable garden. These days it's a popular people place, especially during events like the Canadian Tulip Festival and Colonel By Day on the Civic Holiday in August.

West to Andrew Haydon Park

Start: Find the Champlain Bridge/Ottawa River Parkway parking lot, or lengthen a Parliament Hill Splendour outing by adding this 19-kilometre-return side trip part way along.

Route: An easy cycle along the Ottawa River Parkway.

> **Hint**
> Bring your swimsuit and a picnic.

Sometimes when I need a break from my day-to-day routine, I decide to take an idle cruise down the *Ottawa River Pathway* to enjoy the restful scenery alongside a river that's often monitored closely by seagulls, sailors and swimmers. To do just that, start the cycle west with a cold, refreshing drink from the fountain beside the *Champlain Bridge Parking Lot*. Take the route under the bridge, through the forest, and then left to the spot where the pathway crosses the Ottawa River Parkway. Dismount and walk your bike across the road.

Rejoin the cycling path and begin watching for *Kitchissippi Lookout* in the distance, alongside the river. When you see a knife and fork pointing the way under the bridge to the outdoor restaurant, snack bar and sandy *Westboro Beach*, follow this route, and in the summer expect to find the place abuzz with people enjoying a bit of R and R.

If you've decided to pass up a beach stop for now, continue on the pathway until you reach the stop light at the OC Transpo bus intersection. Cross over and cycle as far as Woodroffe Avenue. From here it's only a bit further until you'll be presented with two options: go straight along the Pinecrest Creek Pathway, or go right to continue cycling on the Ottawa River Pathway. Choose the second alternative and proceed ahead through two tunnels and back to the river's edge.

When you're there, dismount and take a stroll over to the right for a peek at the many waterfowl that frequent the *Deschênes Rapids Lookout Point*. Knowing them, they'll be looking for a handout. Can you see the Britannia Water Filtration Plant off in the distance?

Later, rejoin the pathway and continue west until you reach another intersection. Stay to the right at this point and proceed along to the *Britannia Conservation Area*. Lock your bike up the best you can to explore the informal trails throughout this 48-acre area that make it one of the best bird-watching spots in the capital. If you walk to Mud Lake in May and June look forward to seeing a flush of delicate wild flowers. In the fall, that same forest will be bathed in gold. All in all over 400 plant species and 200 species of birds have been spotted in the conservation area, so there's lots to learn here about the patterns of nature.

Shortly after you leave this region, the pathway crosses Britannia Road. Continue as far as *Britannia Park*. Here you can sunbathe on the beach, swim, picnic, rent a windsurf board or laze about in the sunshine on the breakwater, enjoying Deschênes Lake, a section of the Ottawa River that's two kilometres wide. Notice Lakeside Gardens; it's a community-events complex.

A little further along, past the Belltown Dome Arena, locate *Andrew Haydon Park*, named after a former mayor of Nepean. Although the first settlement began in 1792, it wasn't until 1978 that the area became a city. Today, its population stands about 118,000, and it's part of the mega city of Ottawa. Enjoy the ponds, which are often frequented by remote-control boat owners, the bandstand where outdoor concerts happen each summer, and the barbecues and picnic tables, if need be.

From here, it's only a short distance to some pretty luxurious yachts at the members-only Nepean Sailing Club. Someday, plan to come back and enjoy a cocktail at the clubhouse. This is the turn-around point, so now that you've seen the route highlights, why not zoom back to the Champlain Bridge as fast as you can. Your heart will love you for it!

University to University

Start: Find Tabaret Hall at the University of Ottawa on the corner of Laurier Avenue East and Cumberland Street.
Route: A short section travels uphill on the road. Otherwise, it's primarily a flat cycling path.

Ottawa has three universities. The oldest was founded as St. Joseph's College of Bytown in 1848 by the Roman Catholic bishop Joseph-Bruno Guigues. At that time, five professors taught Greek, Latin, mathematics and religion in classical French style to 60 students in a small, wooden, three-story building on Sussex Drive.

In 1853 Father Joseph-Henri Tabaret, a man who several consider the school's true founder, began heading the institution. The university's academic program really evolved under his leadership, and the numbers attending its English classes in the morning and French in the afternoon increased substantially.

Hints

This one-and-one-half-hour cycle of approximately 14 kilometres is great for Rideau Canal fans. If you park on any side street near the University, a three-hour time limit applies.

Eventually, the college outgrew its downtown space and moved to Sandy Hill, where in 1866 it became the full-fledged *University of Ottawa*, or Ottawa U as it's known locally. Science and mathematics became important parts of the curriculum, and over the years its excellent sports program has seen the Gee-Gees football team win many intercollegiate championships wearing the school colours of garnet and grey.

Today, the administrative offices of North America's oldest bilingual university exist in the ivy-covered, architecturally pleasing *Tabaret Hall*, erected in 1903 after fire destroyed the institution's main building. Leave its expansive lawn via Cumberland Street and cross Laurier Avenue to see where over 24,000 students attend classes taught by a faculty of 1,000.

Continue straight ahead until you come to the T intersection. Turn right and find the road alongside the Morisset Library. Follow this through the campus to the corner of Jean Jacques Lussier and Madame Curie Private. Then it's right, towards the transit way and through the tunnel to Colonel By Drive.

Cross the road and cycle left along the famous *Rideau Canal*, the site of the world's longest skating rink. Just imagine—some of Lieutenant-Colonel John By's 4,500 workers excavated this artificially-cut section of the waterway using shovels and wheelbarrows.

These days, the land on both sides of the water looks much different than it did back in 1855, when Bytown's population was 10,000 and it became the City of Ottawa, a name meaning "traders" in the Algonquin language. For example, when Sir Wilfrid Laurier became Canada's first French-Canadian prime minister he didn't like the look of the place. But by 1899, his dream to have Ottawa take on the beauty he felt the capital city rightly deserved began taking shape. As part of the plan, eyesores along the Rideau Canal were cleaned up, and a driveway suitable for the grand carriages of the day was created along its western edge.

Over the years, on this side of the Rideau Canal, Ottawa's heart became clogged with railroad tracks that converged at the central train station on Wellington Street. In the 1960s, the rails were removed, and Colonel By Drive was established in their place.

Take the second path up to the left to get to the Pretoria Bridge's deck and cross the road at the traffic light. Go over the canal, realizing that when tall boats need to pass, electric motors raise the centre section about two metres. Cycle left at the end of the bridge onto the *Rideau Canal Western Pathway* and head towards Patterson Creek's flowerbeds, which are often ablaze with the red, pink and yellow of the season. Nearby is the Canal Ritz restaurant where First Lady Hillary Clinton, wife of the former United States President, lunched in 1995 after a skate on the Rideau Canal.

Watch for a driveway, and cross Queen Elizabeth Driveway towards *Landsdowne Park*. Named after Canada's Governor General from 1883 to 1888, this park houses the Aberdeen Pavilion, with its cupola-topped turrets and central silver dome. Over the years, this national heritage site served as a military training ground, the spot where William Lyon Mackenzie King won the national Liberal leadership, and home of the Ottawa Senators when they captured the Stanley Cup in 1904. Because livestock were regularly bought, sold and showcased here, the pavilion became known as the "Cattle Castle." Notice the tiny island in the middle of the canal where animals were kept when the exhibition was in full swing.

Elsewhere in the park, the Civic Centre and Frank Clair Stadium provide popular entertainment venues and the August home of the Central Canada Exhibition. The now-defunct Ottawa Roughriders football team played at Landsdowne at one time, with the team winning 9 Grey Cups in 15 before the franchise left the city in 1997. Since 2000, a bubble dome covers the artificial turf from November to May so it may be used for soccer and track and field once the snow flies.

Continue past the orange lilies and fragrant pink roses to get in the mood to view many stately Victorian homes built at the turn of the century by wealthy merchants and federal-government personnel. Pause at *Brown's Inlet* to admire Better-Homes-and-Gardens-like scenes, and then continue along the sidewalk until you reach the informal path leading to the left just before the Bronson Bridge. Take this and proceed to *Commissioners Park*, a place that flourishes with a breathtaking ribbon of colour each May during the Canadian Tulip Festival. In the warm summer months, petunias, daisies and perennials make these spectacular gardens to photograph.

Follow the path that hugs the flowerbeds as far as the traffic lights, and then join the cycling route (marked on the roadway) up the short Prince of Wales Drive hill. Take the road to the right to enjoy a country experience right in the heart of Ottawa at the 1,050-acre *Central Experimental Farm*, which was established in 1886 as a laboratory for agricultural products and innovative farming techniques. Marquis wheat, which was developed here, changed crops forever on the Canadian prairies. Tour some of the roads and paths that crisscross the property among the fields, or stop awhile to admire Dinah, Sophia, Isabela or the pigs, sheep, goats, and poultry that round out the farm's population ($). Call 991-3044, or check out the website www.agriculture.nmstc.ca.

Leave the farm the same way, so you can walk amongst the *Ornamental Garden's* roses, peonies and irises, and the annuals that brighten the land-scape during the summer months. Check out the two hedge collections—

one dates back to the 1890s, while the other was planted in the 1960s.

On the other side of the road and to the right find the seven-hectare *Fletcher Wildlife Garden*, a nature-friendly paradise for birds, butterflies, small mammals and wildflowers, named after the founder of the Ottawa Field Naturalists Club and the Dominion Arboretum's first curator.

Travel back to the traffic circle and into the *Dominion Arboretum*, the place that Fletcher was in charge of. Stop for a botanical, university-type experience, studying the plaques that identify many of the trees and shrubs by their English, French and scientific names.

Retrace your route back down the hill to *Dows Lake*, where several popular events take place during February's Winterlude. The lake exists because Colonel John By and his workers built a dike and a dam at either end of what was once a swamp, to help control water levels and create a navigable body of water during the construction of the canal. Today canoes, paddle boats and in-line skates can be rented at the pavilion.

Cycle right, in front of the *H.M.C.S. Carleton Naval Reserve Building*, following the path gradually left towards the water. Go right where the bulrushes end, right at the path's fork, and then left through another part of the Arboretum. Go left over the small bridge and continue to *Hartwells Locks*, the second station on the Rideau Canal. The grounds here offer a pleasant picnic spot and a chance to watch boats come and go through the hand-operated locks from mid May to mid October. Lift your bike up onto the top lock gate to cross, and then manoeuvre it carefully down the flight of stairs.

Go right here on the bicycle path as far as University Drive at *Carleton University*, a school that has evolved over the past 60-plus years from non-denominational Carleton College to a dynamic, research-intensive university. Cycle straight ahead through the 62-hectare campus that stretches from the Rideau Canal to the Rideau River to see where over 17,000 students learn in more than 50 disciplines. Famous for its journalism school, it also has an outstanding reputation in the fields of public administration and architecture.

Turn left at Campus Avenue and go left along Library Road. Watch for a paved path on the right that offers a chance to go up to Colonel By Drive. Cross the road and you'll be back beside Hartwells Locks once again. Head back towards the University of Ottawa, this time on the *Rideau Canal Eastern Parkway*.

When you reach Pretoria Bridge, detour right on Hawthorne Street, and then right on Main Street if you wish to visit the much-smaller campus of Saint Paul University. This 1,000-student, Catholic, ecumenically oriented institution has united with the University of Ottawa, so its degrees are conferred jointly with that school.

Upon returning to the bike path, if you took the side trip, retrace your route back to the Pretoria Bridge and as far as the next traffic lights. Cross Colonel By Drive to reach the University of Ottawa's campus and the way back to Tabaret Hall. Of interest elsewhere in the National Capital Region, the Université de Québec à Hull, Algonquin College and La Cité Collegiale also provide public post-secondary education.

Sunday Bikedays

Where else in Canada can you cruise carefreely and easily along wide, paved roadways with people as interested in enjoying the outdoors as you are? For over thirty years, thousands of Ottawa's residents and visitors have enjoyed lazy, hazy Sundays on a bike or in-line skates between the May long weekend and Labour Day, on three roads that are closed to vehicular traffic between 9:00 A.M. and 1:00 P.M. To enjoy the first route, gather your gear and the family and start out from downtown Ottawa at the Portage Bridge/Wellington Street intersection. From here, head west along the *Ottawa River Parkway* for nine kilometres, past beautiful waterfront scenery and Westboro Beach, where there is a concession and washrooms. If you wish to park at the Parkway/Champlain Bridge lot, arrive before the roadway closes so you can cycle in either direction from there. In the west end of the city, leave your car at the Lincoln Fields Shopping Centre to access the route from that end.

A second route travels eight kilometres east along the wide-open *Rockcliffe Parkway*, past forests and glimpses of the Ottawa River. Leave your car and cares at the Canadian Aviation Museum parking lot or at the St. Joseph Boulevard/Parkway junction, and the roadway is yours to enjoy.

A third Ottawa Sunday Bikeday option ventures alongside the famous Rideau Canal on *Colonel By Drive*, between Laurier Avenue and Hog's Back Road. Along this eight-kilometre route, which is also ideal for in-line skating, you'll cycle past boaters heading for the Ottawa Locks and Dows Lake. Observe a manually operated lock station in action at either Hartwells or Hog's Back.

On the Quebec side of the Ottawa River, explore *Gatineau Park*'s 40 kilometres of hilly parkways between 6:00 and noon. The Quebec Highway Safety Code allows in-line skating and roller-skiing on the road during Sunday Bikeways, so it's a great occasion to head up through the Gatineau hills to visit places such as Pink Lake, the Champlain Lookout or Penguin Picnic Field this way, instead of on your bike. Parking is available off the Gatineau Parkway at Meech Road, Gamelin Street in Hull, and at the Fortune Lake Parkway, Meech Road intersection.

Two Versions of the Rideau

Start: Between mid May and mid October when the locks are operating, from downtown Ottawa proceed on the marked bike path toward the Alexandra Bridge and go left at the driveway. Look for the Ottawa River Pathway sign. At other times, proceed along Mackenzie Avenue to the Château Laurier Hotel. Turn right and then left onto Elgin Street. Go left at the end of the National War Memorial and cycle down the driveway beside the National Arts Centre. Turn left and travel under the bridge and down the hill.
Route: A confident beginner should be able to handle the steep hills, gradual inclines and lock-gate crossing along this 25-kilometre-plus cycle.

> **Hint**
> Bring some spinach or lettuce to feed the swans—bread harms their digestive tracts.

Experience the exhilaration as you carefully cycle down the very steep, paved incline to the Ottawa River and spectacular views of Parliament Hill, the Canadian Museum of Civilization and the Ottawa Locks.

Find the park bench that I reserved for you to the right of the second lock gate, and sit a bit to think about the history of Canada and to observe the Canadian flag fluttering atop the *Peace Tower*, in what the United Nation's Human Development Index deems to be the best country in the world in which to live.

It was in 1841 that Upper and Lower Canada united to become the Province of Canada. The government met in several cities until 1857 when Queen Victoria named Ottawa the permanent capital. By 1867 the colonies of New Brunswick and Nova Scotia were anxious to join the others in Confederation, so on July 1 of that year the British North America Act was signed, and the Dominion of Canada was born. Sir John A. Macdonald, one of the Fathers of Confederation, became Canada's first prime minister (1867–1873 and 1878–1891). His statue is found on the grounds of Parliament Hill, along with that of Queen Victoria and other famous people who have been instrumental in shaping the country's history.

The *Ottawa Locks* in front of you add to the greatness of this special land. The price to build these giant stairs and the Rideau Canal that links lakes, rivers and canals between here and Lake Ontario was six years of tough manual labour, 823,000 British pounds and hundreds of lives.

During construction, Lieutenant-Colonel John By and the Royal Engineers stocked the supplies and equipment they needed in the stone commissariat storehouse, which operates today as the *Bytown Museum* ($). To have a better look at this 1827 building and have a peek inside to learn more about By, the construction of the canal and the history of early Ottawa, ease your bike up the two stairs onto the lock gate and walk across. The museum's number is 234-4570.

It is said that when Colonel By arrived, there were 150 houses here on the south side of the river. Some were occupied by British Loyalists and veterans of the Napoleonic Wars. Soon, more and more canal builders, lumberjacks and mill workers came to settle, and accommodation was needed for 1,500. By tackled a street plan to determine where new construction should take root. He was a visionary indeed, for his scheme included parkland and a vast space intended for public buildings on what is the now the north side of Wellington Street. Around the lock area, he also mapped out a section so defensive structures could be built to protect the settlement.

Before moving on, look back to see Samuel de Chaplain's statue high atop *Nepean Point*, one of the best viewpoints of this entire historic region. If it's summer, try to attend a concert at the Astrolabe some evening under the stars.

As you cycle left up the hill, perhaps a group of luxurious boats will be entering the locks. The Rideau Canal accommodates recreational vessels 27.4 metres long and 7.9 metres wide that have purchased a lockage permit. It takes about 20 minutes for a vessel to move through each lock gate, most of which are still manually operated. Boaters usually take between three and five days to reach Kingston from here. The time taken depends on how long they tie up along the canal's corridor to soak up its beauty.

Go under the *Plaza Bridge*. Here, during pre-millennium refurbishing, archeologists unearthed remnants of a blacksmith's shop containing tools and other hardware used in the construction of the Rideau Canal, along with footings of the Sapper Bridge, which was also built in 1827.

Across the canal, each day up to 60 Grand Trunk Railway, Canadian Pacific Railway or Canadian National Railway trains used to roll into Ottawa's *Union Station*. Since 1967, when the station relocated, this impressive building has been the scene of many federal-provincial and international government conferences. Plans are now underway to make it the Canadian Sports Hall of Fame.

Detour up the steep concrete pathway to view the *National War Memorial*, where Canada's Remembrance Day service is held each November 11 at 11:00 A.M. The Response features 22, 2.5-metre figures pushing forward, with hope and determination, under the guidance of Peace and Freedom. All branches of the service are represented. In May 2000, the remains of an unknown Canadian soldier killed during the First World War were moved to the three-tiered granite sarcophagus from France's Vimy Ridge.

Back on the *Rideau Canal Western Pathway*, you'll see the *National Arts Centre*, whose four impressive venues showcase orchestra, dance and English and French theatre. It's along this stretch of the canal that each July 1 boaters deck their vessels out in flags and red-and-white paraphernalia and tie up to celebrate Canada's birthday. This spot also marks the termination of the flotilla, a parade of colourful boats held during May's Canadian Tulip

Festival, and of the wintertime skating freeway, which extends the length of 200 Olympic-size hockey rinks to Dows Lake.

On the right, the red-brick Cartier Square Drill Hall serves as home to two infantry regiments—the Governor-Generals Foot Guard and the Cameron Highlanders of Ottawa. The nearby headquarters administers services for the City of Ottawa's 791,000 citizens.

As you cycle around the curve, stop and look back to see the campus of the *University of Ottawa*. On the right, watch for the German Embassy, one of over a hundred such ambassadorial buildings in Canada's capital. Follow the path closest to Queen Elizabeth Driveway as you approach the Pretoria Bridge, and cross over its deck to the *Rideau Canal Eastern Pathway*. Before long, the Aberdeen Pavilion and Frank Clair Stadium in *Landsdowne Park* will come into view.

As you pass *Dows Lake*, imagine seeing skaters gliding along the ice on a sunny winter afternoon. During the Tulip Festival, thousands of bulbs bloom in the gardens of Commissioners Park across the lake; later in the season, colourful annuals and perennials flourish instead.

On your left is *Carleton University*, famous for its journalism and administration programs, and on the right are the *Hartwells* and *Hog's Back Lock Stations*. All in all, there are 24 of these on the canal corridor, with a total of 49 locks.

Cycle under the bridge to find the *Rideau Canoe Club*, where sprint racing is popular. Here each June, the National Capital Dragon Boat Festival provides a golden opportunity to watch 3,500 paddlers race brightly-painted, 12-metre vessels. Look off in the distance for *Mooney's Bay*, a favourite Ottawa spot for swimming and cross-country skiing. Each July the beach attracts 10,000 players for the largest charity volleyball tournament in the world.

Detour along the water's edge and under the bridge to the spot where Colonel By decided that vessels would never be able to navigate the treacherous *Hog's Back Falls*, let alone the ones at the spot where the Rideau River tumbles into the Ottawa. Have a look for yourself, and soak up some negative ions as the water roars over the rocks leaving a path of frothing lace.

Cycle back to where the Rideau River parts, and take the path that leads up and over the bridge deck and past the private marina. Continue through the tunnel under the bridge into Hog's Back Park and go left to enjoy the falls from a whole new perspective.

When you've seen enough, take one of the paved paths a short distance up to the parking lot and locate the *Rideau River Eastern Pathway*. Follow it through the forest until it's time to slow down, as the route snakes down a steep hill and into the 28.9-hectare *Vincent Massey Park*. Named after Canada's governor general from 1952–1959, continue your escape from urban life as squirrels scamper, birds sing and the forest stands silently watching you pass.

Hog's Back Falls

Look for the *Rideau River*, as opposed to the Rideau Canal, showing through the trees, and another part of the Carleton University campus across the babbling water. Anytime now, and particularly around the parking lot area beside the path, you may find elegant black or white swans, or families of ducks looking for the greens you brought.

Across Riverside Drive, notice the Recreational Association Centre, where public servants gather to play hockey and tennis and to curl. Cross Bank Street at the Billings Bridge intersection and after about a block, look across the grass for the traffic light/blue sign pointing the way to the *Billings Estate Museum* ($). Cut across the lawn and go up Pleasant Park hill and right to take a self-guided tour of the oldest house in Ottawa and heirlooms belonging to the family of American-born Braddish Billings, who worked awhile on the Rideau Canal. While there, lock up your bike and have a look at the lilies and the irises, the gatehouse and smokehouse, and the cemetery where 140 of the area's first settlers were buried. For more information, call 247-4830.

Return to the cycling path and continue towards the Smyth Road Bridge. Watch for the Riverside Hospital on your right, one of three campuses that comprise the Ottawa Hospital. Soon the path moves away from Riverside Drive and plunges into the cool, canopied woods again, before passing under Highway 417, or the Queensway as it is known.

Between here and the Cummings Bridge, the paved path divides the pastoral river front from the expansive green lawns where children play and picnic. Along the way, the private Rideau Tennis Club fronts the path close to the spot where Strathcona Park appears across the river. It's in this spot that Odyssey presents its popular, month-long, live-theatre production each summer.

Cross Montreal Road and continue through the beautiful, well-maintained riverside parks and the tunnel under the St. Patrick's Bridge. Here the path turns to packed earth for a short while, as it moves through New Edinburgh Park, past its tennis courts and on towards the Minto Bridges and eventually Sussex Drive.

Cross the drive and locate the *Canada and the World Pavilion* that show-cases the achievements of Canadians on the world stage. Nearby, take a look at *Rideau Falls*, the second reason Colonel By knew that boats could never make it from the Rideau River into the Ottawa. Come back after dark to see these waterfalls, named by explorer Samuel de Champlain, illuminated from behind with coloured lights.

From here, travel on Sussex Drive toward Green Island and the City of Ottawa's former city hall, designed by Moshe Safdie, who also designed the National Gallery. The building on the right is occupied by the *National Research Council*, a federal organization that conducts studies at its Ottawa locations in areas ranging from aerospace to hydraulics and thermal technology.

Next door is *Earnscliffe*, the home of the British high commissioner to Canada, and once the home of Sir John A. Macdonald. Across the road, the *Lester B. Pearson Building* serves as headquarters for Canada's Foreign Service. Just past the Macdonald-Cartier Bridge overpass, the embassies of Saudi Arabia and Japan dominate the landscape a short distance before the *Royal Canadian Mint*. Here, the mint produces the country's collector coins, medallions, medals, and gold, platinum and silver maple-leaf bullion coins. Call 993-8990 or 1-800-276-7714, or visit www.rcmint.ca.

Next door at the *Canadian War Museum*, within a First World War trench, one gets a feel of how the war's devastation affected mothers, fathers, sisters, brothers, wives, husbands, sweethearts and children. Call 776-8600, or go to www.warmuseum.ca.

Nearby, the *National Gallery of Canada's* glass pinnacle pierces the Ottawa skyline. Masterpieces by the Group of Seven and the Rideau Street Convent Chapel are showcased as part of its extensive Canadian collection. Call 990-1985, or check out www.national.gallery.ca.

Before ending your outing, *Notre-Dame Basilica's* beautiful twin spires will encourage you to take a look inside the oldest surviving church in Ottawa, to see its awe-inspiring, star-studded ceiling and ornately decorated interior.

Kitty–corner from the church, take particular note of the *National Peacekeeping Monument*, another reminder of why Canada is such a great place to live. In 1988, the awarding of the Nobel Peace Prize to the UN peacekeepers inspired Canada to erect The Reconciliation, in honour of the men and women who served to restore peace in war-torn lands around the world.

Famous Residences and People

Start: From downtown Ottawa, travel along Sussex Drive to John Street to locate New Edinburgh's first school.

Route: About 15 kilometres of mostly on-road travel. Some steep hills.

Ottawa is known for its fancy neighborhoods and famous people, partly because of its role as Canada's capital. Find out where some of its foreign ambassadors live, and then add influences from the city's historic past along with a touch of the economic impact today's high-tech industry has had on the area, and you have the perfect itinerary for an interesting cycle along New Edinburgh and Rockcliffe Park streets.

Hints
Call ahead to find out when you can tour the RCMP stables. Drive this route instead if you feel like it.

Get on your bike at the old stone two-story *New Edinburgh School*, where some of the children of the rich and famous are sure to have learned to read and write, and turn right onto Sussex Drive. Notice the High Commission of South Africa on your right. Throughout Ottawa there are 120 diplomatic missions from countries ranging from Algeria to Zimbabwe, and almost 1,000 associated households. On this outing, you'll see many of their colourful flags flying. Try to identify them as you go.

But first, turn right at the corner and expect to see the Canadian flag fluttering in the breeze at *7 Rideau Gate*, Canada's official guesthouse. Distinguished visitors stay here regularly so that they are close to the prime-minister's home and the governor-general's residence straight ahead. Enter the estate's grounds, and follow the driveway up to *Rideau Hall*. Thomas MacKay, the Scottish masonry entrepreneur who built the lower eight locks of the Rideau Canal, created this mansion in 1838. His work there and at other places around Bytown obviously paid well!

Thirty years later, the Canadian government purchased the two-story, eleven-room property to be a home for its governor general. Over the years, various additions have been made. An indoor tennis court, which converted to a beautiful spot for evening dinner parties once striped fabric was draped on the walls, enlarged the mansion in the 1870s. About the same time, an elegant ballroom became available for parties, music and dance events.

Today, the governor general uses this room for official functions. It is his or her duty as the Queen's representative and Canada's head of state to swear in the government's cabinet, bestow Canada's highest honours, and welcome dignitaries from around the world, many of whom plant trees on the property to commemorate their visit. When the governor general is in residence, the blue standard flies.

Take a tour of the public rooms if they're open to guests, ask to be shown where there's public skating in the winter, and then head back down the driveway of this national historic site to see the inukshuk, an Inuit stone marker that more commonly stands on the Arctic's frozen landscape.

Take time to smell the fragrance of almost 300 varieties of roses in the *Canadian Heritage Garden*, while studying the inscriptions that chronicle important historical dates from 1608 to 1992 and recognize Canada's diverse cultural influences. Exit through Rideau Hall's main gate, past the spot where the Relief of the Sentry takes place each summer. Turn right and proceed cautiously on the road down the hill to the end of the 32-hectare property. For more information call 991-4422 or 1-866-842-4422, or visit www.gg.ca.

Cross the road to reach the *Ottawa River Pathway* and proceed as far as Buena Vista Road. Leave the cycling path here and go straight up bumpy Lisgar Road into the heart of the prestigious Rockcliffe Park neighbourhood, which was still its own village until municipal restructuring added it to Ottawa's fold in 2001. Notice that there are no sidewalks and no stores; the only amenities available to its 2,000 citizens are a library and three schools.

On your way up the hill, watch for *500 Lisgar Road*, the ambassadorial compound of the United States of America, which is definitely the place to be for the big Fourth of July party if you have an invitation. When you're downtown sometime, look for the large, grey United States Embassy on Mackenzie Avenue across from Major's Hill Park.

At the end of the estate, follow narrow, maple-lined Rockcliffe Road up past the Indonesian ambassador's residence to the *Pope's Nuntiatura Apostolica* at 724 Manor Avenue. The arched gateway provides a great chance to have a peek at this magnificent home that the Vatican bought in 1962.

Continue along to Coltrin Road, turn right and then follow Coltrin and Minto Place as far as Soper Place. Go right. Believe it or not, the core of the magnificent home on the corner, at 299, belonging to the founder of the high-technology company Cognos, was once a stable.

Follow the other sightseers straight ahead to *234 Perley Court*, to see where two of Ottawa's most famous citizens reside in their $10-million, 10,000-square-foot, copper-coloured mansion. Michael Cowpland, whose firm Corel took the world by storm with Corel Draw, lives here with his wife Marlen, who makes her mark in the world with her revealing high fashion and love of animals.

Retrace your route to Minto, turn right and continue to Buena Vista Road. Go left past the private *Elmwood School*, attended by boys and girls from kindergarten to grade 3, and girls from grades 4–13. Canada's first female senator, Cairine Wilson, served as its head girl years ago, and Princess Beatrix studied there in the 1940s. Turn left immediately after the school, onto Springfield Road, and continue until you see the huge red-brick home belonging to the German ambassador to Canada on the corner at 290 Coltrin Road. Go right here and then left to 725 Acacia Avenue to have a better look at the elegant stone residence of the Japanese envoy.

To get a spectacular vista of the Ottawa River and Kettle Island, continue down Acacia to the park bench. I hope you brought a snack and a drink. Later, find the paved path that goes into the *Rockcliffe Rockeries*, a popular place for wedding photos and relaxation amid the well-landscaped gardens. Look for the columns from the old Ottawa Public Library, which was demolished in the 1970s.

Poke around and enjoy the gardens as you like, and then go right at the path's Y intersection and up the hill to Acacia Avenue. Use this road as your base to explore the neighbourhood on your own for as long as you wish. On Acacia itself, watch for the home of the Spanish ambassador to Canada (on the left at Crescent Road), with its gigantic flag out front, and *Stornoway* at 541, purchased in 1970 by the Canadian government to be a home for the leader of the official opposition in the House of Commons. Check out the homes of the neighbours, who hail from Iraq, India, Korea, and Thailand.

If you want to see *Ashbury College*, a private junior and senior high school, detour right at Buchan Road. Go left in front of the school on Mariposa Avenue and then head back to Acacia.

At the end of your explorations, locate the corner of Acacia Avenue and Oakhill Road, about four blocks past Buena Vista Road on the left. Turn here and go slowly down the steep hill. Go left onto Beechwood Avenue and ahead a very short distance to the entrance of the 160-acre *Beechwood Cemetery*.

Established in 1873, this ecumenical and bilingual burial place opened at the time of the area's lumber boom. In 2001, it was named Canada's National Military Cemetery. Many other historically significant Canadians also rest here. For example, the gazebo, to the right of the administrative office, contains the ashes of Tommy Douglas, a Canadian socialist who served as premier of Saskatchewan before becoming the first leader of the National Democratic Party in 1961.

Check out the panoramic view of Parliament Hill and then get "lost" looking for the tombstones of famous people like Sir Robert Borden, who was Canada's prime minister from 1911–1920. Look for the historical graves of John Rodolphus Booth, who once owned the largest lumber mill in the world at Chaudière Falls, and Sir Sanford Fleming, chief surveyor of the Canadian Pacific Railway and man behind the idea of standard time. Elsewhere, Sir Cecil Spring Rice, the man who wrote one of the hymns sung at Princess Diana's funeral, rests in peace. He passed away while in Canada visiting the governor general.

If you know Ottawa at all, you'll recognize that Cooper, Slater, Sparks, Smyth, Sweetland and Bronson all have city streets named after them. See if you can find graves of some of the members of the original Ottawa Senators hockey team, or members of the Northwest Mounted Police, before heading back to the cemetery's entrance.

Turn right here onto Beechwood-Hemlock and travel on the road as far as Birch Avenue. Go left and proceed along this residential street and across Sandridge Road. At the sign, turn right to see the impressive home of some very famous horses—those of the *Royal Canadian Mounted Police's Musical Ride*. Even if the 32-rider precision troupe is on tour, continue straight ahead during the hours when the stable is open to the public to see the horses that are in residence. Call 993-3751, or visit www.rcmp-grc.gc.ca.

Later, leave the property and go right on Birch Avenue. Carefully cross over the Rockcliffe Parkway to the Ottawa River Pathway on the other side,

Government Landau on display at the RCMP Stables.

and go left towards the Ottawa New Edinburgh Boat Club. Get prepared for a steep ascent up the winding hill; ride on the sidewalk as the road is narrow. Stop at the *lookout point* on top for great views of the Ottawa River and the City of Gatineau, Quebec.

If you want to rent a four-person pontoon for a trip up to Parliament Hill or relax awhile beside the water over a sandwich or plate of nachos, go down the steep driveway to the Rockcliffe Boathouse Restaurant. Otherwise, go straight ahead and take a side trip right along the road into *Rockcliffe Park* itself for a great view of the back of the prime minister's and French ambassador's residences. This cool tree-covered oasis also affords a special place for picnics, family reunions and impromptu jam sessions.

Continue the loop through the park and then go right onto the cycling path until you see the governor general's estate once more. On your right now, take a close-up look at the prime minister's residence at *24 Sussex Drive*. Built in 1868 by a wealthy mill owner, this prestigious address that Canadians hear about often has been that of many of the men whose statues appear on the grounds of Parliament Hill. It seems a perfect location to end a famous-people-and-residences tour, so from here head back toward your vehicle along Sussex Drive, past the home of the French ambassador to Canada.

Ottawa River Solitude

Start: Locate the first parking lot on the Rockcliffe Parkway past the New Edinburgh Boat Club.
Route: Easy, as the majority of this 23-kilometre trail is flat.

Sometimes in today's busy world, one needs to switch their mind onto automatic pilot and chill out awhile away from it all. The Ottawa River's shoreline offers just the perfect spot.

> **Hint**
> Makes a perfect just-me-and-my-shadow kind of outing for a couple of hours.

To get started, go right towards downtown Ottawa from the parking lot to find the path marked Hillsdale Road. Cycle down the hill to the well-maintained stone-dust *Ottawa River Pathway*, and check if a group of new sailors are having a lesson at the marvellous, circa 1920s Ottawa New Edinburgh Boat Club, a private sailing and tennis club.

From here, cycle right and immediately begin turning your troubles into mere blips on your radar screen as you put your bike in easy pedalling gear and your mind in neutral. As you cycle for long periods along the shaded path, with only the water licking the rocks and the leaves rustling nearby, the bike's rhythm makes this kind of a moving meditation.

After a fair stretch, the path reaches the private *Rockcliffe Yacht Club*. Stop awhile and watch the boaters come and go, and the occasional small plane that has taken off from the Rockcliffe Airport up the hill. If it's a hot day, a cold drink from the club's soft-drink machine can be a life saver.

Before long, the path passes the public boat launch. In these parts, expect that speedboats may interrupt your solitude. As you continue, ignore any roads or paths that lead up the hill to marked destinations, and instead enjoy the relaxing water scenery and the colourful wildflowers that brighten the landscape.

Eventually, the path leads up to the right, and through the cool, dense forest that forms part of Ottawa's Greenbelt. Cross the bridge on the sidewalk to find the path soon plunging back into the woods and left, back towards the river. If it's summer, before long you'll be whizzing past fields of corn and a magnificent and fragrant meadow of wild flowers that unfolds as you arrive on the edge of the former city of *Orleans*, a bedroom community about 15 to 20 minutes by car from downtown.

Proceed ahead along Rosslyn Street, and follow the path until eventually the trail comes to the wetlands, where children love to catch tadpoles in the shadows alongside the path. Stop and make a whistle from a blade of grass before heading for the end of the cycling path at 10th Line Road.

Turn around here for the tranquil 11.5-kilometre cycle back. On the way, have a look for Quebec's Kettle Island in the Ottawa River. Rather than taking

An afternoon cycle beside the Ottawa River.

the same path up to your car, take the one marked Birch Avenue for a change of scene. Once at the top, go right back to the parking lot, hopefully feeling so rested that you don't want to leave these peaceful surroundings.

Lunch and a Swim in Aylmer

Start: From downtown Hull, drive along Laurier Street and Alexandre-Taché Boulevard as far as Boudria Street (immediately left at the second traffic light after the sign for the Gatineau Park Entrance). Go left, to leave your car at Mousette Park.
Route: An easy, well-maintained, paved route for about 90 percent of its 40 kilometres. The rest is rolling hills encountered in the last stretch through Gatineau Park.

Hints
Bring your swimsuit. Pack a picnic or plan to eat at Aylmer's marina.

A leisurely cycle in somewhat idyllic surroundings and a tasty lunch and swim are a welcome respite and reward after days of museum going, Parliament Hill sightseeing, or a hectic week at the office.

To begin the circuit that has Aylmer as its primary destination, join the *Voyageurs Pathway* and cycle from *Mousette Park* to the right, away from Hull, on a section of the paved route that often skirts the lush, shady forest. Keep alert at all times for others—in-line skaters love it—sharing this smooth path as you journey to see the water boiling at the Petit Chaudière Rapids. Keep left and follow the path along the river that goes under the Champlain Bridge.

Before long, you'll pass the manicured greens of the Château Cartier golf course, and a wealth of golden, purple and dusty-pink wildflowers if it's summer. The fresh scent of the forest invites you to package some to take home. At the river's edge, a couple of viewpoints off the beaten track allow a glimpse of Parliament Hill in the distance, and the Kitchissippi Lookout and Westboro Beach Park across on the Ontario side of the river.

Stop at the turbulent *Deschênes Rapids* to see where an electricity-generating station once powered lumber and flour mills, and the electric railway that ran between Aylmer and Hull/Ottawa. These treacherous waters still block today's boaters from travelling down the Ottawa River highway to the St. Lawrence, in the same way they did Samuel de Champlain and aboriginal fur traders hundreds of years ago. Did you ever consider the impact these rapids and the Hog's Back and Rideau Falls have had on the nation's capital?

By the way, that's the Britannia Yacht Club and Britannia Beach that you see across the water, as you leave the rapids to cycle along the path that soon passes beside Lucerne Boulevard and on through a residential area into

Aylmer. It's around this spot that many early Ottawa River travellers stopped to explore and rest after a long journey. In 1832 a stone hotel opened to accommodate steamship passengers who passed this far along the river up until the end of the century; today the old Symmes Inn, on the right where the pathway crosses the road, operates as the city's cultural centre. Nearby, in the Parc de l'Imaginaire, have a look at the art in the park. Perhaps musicians will be entertaining.

Over the years, the City of Aylmer laid claim to being the legal and political centre for this part of Quebec. Its court and prison are the first this side of Montreal. Originally the citizens were primarily Anglophones, as most lumber barons emigrated from the British Isles; today, it's the bilingual home of 35,000.

Take a detour up the main street for a quick look at some of the stately Victorian homes, and then continue on the Voyageurs Pathway past the marina to the *Parc Des Cèdres* beach. Go for a swim to work up an appetite, and if you brought the young ones in a bike trailer, take them to the playground. Later, munch on your picnic eats, or head back to the marina's restaurant for a scrumptious lunch alongside what is the widest section of the Ottawa River in these parts. Between its Quebec and Ontario shores, Lac Deschênes provides a two-kilometre-wide expanse for sailing and windsurfing.

After you've eaten, follow the Voyageurs Pathway again, this time past the beach and water's edge to Lattion Road. Follow the yellow line along the pathway for several blocks as it moves up and north to the *Pionniers Pathway*. Cross the road where indicated, and then put your mind in neutral. Here's a great chance to work off a few calories if you ate too much, as the route parallels Highway 148 East for about ten kilometres, past Aylmer homes, the forest, grasslands and meadows of delicate flowers. For most of the summer, the sight of hundreds of goldenrod makes this whole trip worthwhile.

When the pathway ends, follow *Des Grides Road* left as far as the traffic light at Chemin de la Montagne. Turn left up this busy street onto the Voyageurs Pathway (on the left side of the road) until you reach the third set of traffic lights beside the fire hall. Cross the road to join up with a short section of the *Lac-des-Feés Pathway* that takes you east to the *Gatineau Park Pathway*. Slow and steady does it here, as the path meanders gently up and down through dense woods for a couple of kilometres towards the end of this cycling circle. Remember to shift gears!

Before long, you'll be at the *Gatineau Park Entrance* on Alexandre-Taché Boulevard. Go right here to the second traffic light and then left to locate your car at Mousette Park. I bet you'll sleep well tonight!

Mountain Biking

Whenever I see bikers standing on their pedals as they challenge the mountain terrain, it reminds me of the rodeo cowboys at the Calgary Stampede. If you are one of these thrill seekers, load up your wheels and head for the hills to test your skill and balance atop your mount on some spectacular trails. A great place to get started at this increasingly popular sport is *Gatineau Park*. Ninety kilometres of scenic terrain sit waiting to dare mountain-bike enthusiasts to enjoy the wonders of nature on well-marked shared trails between May 15 and November 30.

Before setting out, purchase a Gatineau Park Summer Trail Map ($) at the visitors centre on Scott Road in Old Chelsea, or at the Capital Infocentre across from Parliament Hill to help locate the parking lots (P) and to learn the difficulty of the various trails and which paths are designated for hiking or biking use. Throughout this and every other mountain-biking area, respect all "No Bicycles" signs. If you cycle on these trails, consider any environmental damage to be permanent. And as a lover of the outdoors, I'm sure you don't want that.

If you haven't had time to pick up a map, here are a few trails to try. An easy route to get you started begins at P16. Make sure to pack your towel, swimsuit and a picnic, as you're off via Trail 50 to Lac Phillippe for the day. Along the way, you'll pass Herridge Shelter, where you can stop for a rest if need be. Head back the same way. On a second trip out, try this trip that includes a wide variety of topography. Beginning at P7, take Trail 30 up a steep slope for about a kilometre until you reach the junction with Trail 1. From here you're off to the races once you head left in the direction of Keogan Shelter, and continue onwards over the rolling hills until you come to the Champlain Lookout. Have a peek at the panoramic view, and then rejoin Trail 1 if you're up to it, for a much more demanding cycle as far as the fire tower. Retrace your path back to your vehicle.

Another time, experience the thrill of cycling in a part of Gatineau Park that's farther north. Park at P17 and take Trail 53 and Trail 51 as far as the road leading to Lac Philippe. Go left on the road to reach the beach and a chance to relax awhile. Later, complete the loop back to your vehicle by taking Trail 50 and then Trail 52 left, which is part of the Trans Canada Trail. Count on this being a long day!

A last idea is something for those seeking a more technically challenging route. Park at P11 at Meech Lake's O'Brien Beach, and be prepared to really test your mountain-biking skills along Trail 36. Eventually, you'll come to Trail 50, which is a much easier trail; take it left if you want to add some more cycling time to your outing before heading back to your car. For information call 819-827-2020, or visit www.capcan.ca.

Another alternative if you're looking for something challenging is to try Gatineau Park's *Camp Fortune*. Plan on 20 kilometres of intermediate to advanced trails that will test your technical, obstacle-dodging, and cross-county abilities. National and international races take place here for those adept at this sport; sign up for lessons or the learn-to-race program if you're not so confident. From Hull, take Highway 5 North to Exit 12 for Old Chelsea. Turn left and continue through the village and onto Meech Lake Road. Watch for the signs. For Camp Fortune info call 819-827-1717 or 1-888-283-1717, or go to www.campfortune.com.

If you don't mind adding a leisurely one-way drive of about 90 minutes to your cycling day, consider using your bike to climb the mountains across from the tourist information centre in *Montebello*. Ask the staff for a map of the more "natural" intermediate to expert trails before setting out. The phone number is 819-423-5602.

Another time, take two to three hours to drive to *Mont Tremblant* to flex your muscles on 40 kilometres of paths rated from easy to expert. Pick up a map at the information centre to locate the Jack Rabbit, Pine, Labyrinth and Devils routes, so you can test your mountain-biking skills with the best of them. For more information call 819-681-2000 or 1-888-736-2526, or check out www.tremblant.ca.

P'tit Train du Nord Linear Park

Start: From Hull, take Highway 50 and Highway 148 East to Montebello, and Highway 323 North to St-Jovite. Go left on Highway 117 North until the exit for La Conception/Mont Tremblant (eight kilometres past St-Jovite). Proceed straight on Tulips Road towards Mont Tremblant/Labelle as far as Les Jardins de l'Achillée Millefeuille (number 4352).
Route: Easy, as the average slope of the packed, stone-chip trail is 2 percent.

Hints
Complete this 55-kilometre-plus return trip in a day, or stay overnight to soak up more of the ambiance of the Laurentians. Bike rentals are available in most villages.

When you cycle any part of the 200-kilometre *P'tit Train du Nord Linear Park* trail between St. Jérôme and Mount Laurier, picture a train full of mountain-air lovers travelling the same route back in the 1930s. They came back then, particularly from Montreal, to hike and swim in the summer, ski in the winter, and holiday in the villages that sprang up along the train's route through the Laurentians.

Once the passenger trains stopped operating in 1981 and shipping of freight ended eight years later, it was time to find a new use for this picturesque rail corridor. In 1996, with tracks removed, the rail bed was transformed into a smooth path. Along the way, the train stations and bridges were also rebuilt so trail users would feel like they were still riding the rails.

Since its rebirth, over a million cyclists, walkers, cross-country skiers, and snowmobilers have used the recreational pathway. Among these are individuals, families, and a blind gentleman and his sighted companion who cycled the route end-to-end. Enthusiasts make the return trip; others rely on a taxi to take them back to their starting point.

Begin a day's adventure at any of the towns and villages along the trail on board a touring or hybrid bicycle with a season linear-park pass ($) in hand. Get one from the trail patrol, or at any Laurentian Tourist Information Centre. At these offices, secure a map listing attractions and accommodation along the entire route, and get help, if need be, with your itinerary planning. Call 1-800-561-6673, or go to www.laurentides.com.

Here is one suggestion for a leisurely R-and-R-type outing along the route that includes sightseeing stops along the way and an overnight in the Laurentians. Begin at Jardins de l'Achillée Millefeuille, a health centre right on the bike path just north of *La Conception* at the trail's 97.4-kilometre mark. Great food, beautiful gardens, and B and B or Indian teepee accommodation make this a popular place with cyclists. For information call 819-686-9187.

After a refreshing fruit drink, head south about six kilometres to the old train station at the village of *Mont Tremblant*, on the shores of Lac Mercier (it's now an art gallery with many historical photos of the train era). Detour left here onto the paved recreational trail up the mountain to spend some time discovering what brings thousands to the *Mont Tremblant Resort Area* annually. Among other attractions, there's the beach at Lac Tremblant, 30 kilometres of hiking routes with paths ranging from easy to strenuous, many kilometres of technically challenging mountain-bike trails, plus lots of fine eateries, great cookies and a microbrewery.

After you've had a chance to do some exploring, head back to the P'tit Train du Nord Linear Park route again and continue south to *Les Terrasses du Lac*, just past the 81-kilometre mark. Enjoy a snack or light meal, the colourful gardens and the view of Black Creek, all from the comfort of an Adirondack chair. Without a doubt, this is the life!

If you're planning to include an overnight stay, the charming resort village of St-Jovite is a great place to find accommodation, boutiques and fabulous dining. Cycle into town by leaving the path at Labelle to look for a place to stay, or better still, book ahead to enjoy the inviting B-and-B hospitality offered at Trigonelle, at 819-425-9575, right on the bike path, or Le Second Souffle at 819-429-6166, close by. From either, it's not far to travel into the village for dinner later on.

When its time to move on, cycle south past hundreds of wildflowers to visit the former provincially operated *Fish Hatchery* ($) at St-Faustin. Today, the village maintains tanks of young fish and farm animals, with a special place set aside to land "the big one." If you're lucky, get the fish cleaned on the spot so you can savour it fresh after it's cooked at the nearby outdoor restaurant.

From here, the trail moves gradually uphill until it reaches the old *train station at St-Faustin Lac Carré*. Sneak a peek inside before cycling down Main Street about two blocks for a swim at the public beach.

Later in the day, the 27-kilometre return trip to La Conception is heavenly. What goes up must come down, so sit back in the saddle and relax while enjoying the vegetation, lakes, and lazy butterflies that call this place home.

On future cycling trips along the linear park trail, consider an outing in the Lake Nominique area, about 50 kilometres farther north. Other cyclists report that the forest and lakes in this area are exquisitely beautiful. Another popular option is the 25-kilometre trip farther south from St-Agathe des Monts to St-Adèle, a great four-season resort village.

Note: In the winter back in the 1940s, visitors also came by "Snow Train" to the Laurentians to enjoy the outdoors. These days if you return between December 1 and April 15, you can cross-country ski on the most southerly 42 kilometres of the linear park trail from St-Jérôme to Val-David, or snow-mobile on the rest of the route if this is your preferred way to "ride the rails."

PPJ Cycloparc

Start: From downtown Hull, take Highway 148 West (drive left along Laurier Street, Alexandre-Taché and Aylmer Road. Turn right at Park Street and then onto Eardley Road) and proceed towards Wyman and the beginning of the Cycloparc.

Route: Off-road travel on a packed, fine-gravel path with a grade of 4 percent.

> **Hint**
> Bring along a hybrid or mountain bike, sunscreen, and a picnic to enjoy at one of the tables beside the trail.

Pontiac country lies in a beautiful but largely undiscovered part of Quebec, located between the Ottawa River and the Laurentian Plateau. Cycling along the 72-kilometre *PPJ Cycloparc* will acquaint you with this picturesque area that served as the hunting ground for the Algonquins hundreds of years ago.

In the seventeenth century, the Ottawa River, named Kichesippi or Great River after one of the Algonquin tribes, became a highway to move precious furs and beaver pelts downstream by birch canoe to trade with the French and Europeans. In time, forts and trading posts sprang up along the route, and the forest industry began. More and more white settlers arrived, and soon log drives became a common sight on the mighty waterway.

Years later, it was decided that a railroad would be the best way to carry lumber, wheat, farm produce and passengers between Aylmer and Waltham. The Canadian Pacific's Pontiac Pacific Junction Railway, or "Push, Pull and Jerk Railway," did the job. By 1984, however, roads had become the primary transportation choice, so the tracks and ties were removed between Wyman and Waltham, and part of the original rail line became the PPJ Cycloparc recreational pathway.

On the way to the route's beginning, notice the spectacular *Eardley Escarpment* that forms the southwestern boundary of Gatineau Park. On the other side of the road, catch a glimpse of where the Ottawa River widens to become Lac des Chats, reputed to be a great spot to land a catfish.

Pass the signs pointing to the village of Quyon, and begin watching for the large brown-and-green *PPJ Cycloparc sign* at Wyman Road. Stop to decide if this is the place to launch your adventure. For discussion purposes, I've divided the trail into four sections of about equal length, with each part ending at a delightful Pontiac town where you can explore, have something to eat or even stay over at a B and B, inn or campground. Along the way, interesting side trips will allow you to learn more about this special part of Quebec. Call 1-800-665-5217, or visit www.cycloparcppj.org.

Because the trail is primarily flat, any excursion makes a perfect family outdoor activity. Take care though not to skid on the fine gravel, and set out early in the day, as many parts of the route are without shade. Markers in kilometres along the trail make it easy for you to track the distance cycled.

To *start at zero kilometres*, leave your car near the PPJ Cycloparc sign along Highway 148, and cycle to the intersection of Wyman and Gold Mine Road. From here the recreational path meanders through lush forests resplendent with wildflowers and beside ponds and rich agricultural land. Along the way watch for evidence of the 1998 ice storm and interpretation panels describing the area's history and ecology.

When you reach *Shawville*, 16.5 kilometres away, the region's primary healthcare centre—the Pontiac Community Hospital—will be on the right. On the other side are the fairgrounds that play host each Labour Day weekend to a popular agricultural fair that's been held since 1856. Nearby, catch a glimpse into the past at the old PPJ train station.

If this is your destination for this outing, cycle left on Centre Street to take a look around the area before heading back. Photos indicate that Shawville's business core looks much as it did 100 years ago, with many of the impressive buildings built using bricks from the two factories that once operated here. If you're English-speaking, you'll be right at home in most of the Pontiac, and particularly in this area.

To begin cycling on the *second stretch of the path*, park near Shawville's fairgrounds and begin the 19-kilometre journey to Campbell's Bay. Wetlands, a peat bog, forests and great views of the countryside present themselves, along with wildlife, birds and livestock grazing in the fields.

In *Campbell's Bay*, the route passes close to the water along Front Street, where many businesses are located. The PPJ Railway Station is gone, but several of the other original buildings still exist in this town that boasts the region's courthouse and administrative headquarters. Have a look around before setting out back to Shawville.

If you would rather cycle the *third section of the Cycloparc*, park at Campbell's Bay and ride through forests and past the farm fields that front the 18-kilometre path between the Ottawa River and the lush green mountainsides on the way to Fort Coulonge. Keep your eyes peeled for wildlife.

Plan to leave the trail at Baume Street in *Fort Coulonge* for some sightseeing. Proceed through town and turn right onto Principale Street to enjoy the peaceful ambiance of this charming stretch that runs along beside the Coulonge River. The magnificent stone houses at numbers 200, 204 and 224 once belonged to the Bryson children. George Bryson, their father, came to the area in 1835 to look at lumbering prospects. Over time, he became both a local and provincial politician, and with others, founded the Bank of Ottawa in 1874.

Continue along the road to the *Marchand Bridge*. This 129-metre beauty was constructed in 1898 to provide a quick route to Fort Coulonge from the lumbering camps. Today, it's a designated Quebec historic site because of its fine architectural qualities. It's fun to cycle through this pine structure—be careful, it's one-way traffic—to take a photo on the other side. When you're there, take a side trip a short way right along Highway 148 to tour George Bryson's family home before turning back and rejoining the Cycloparc path where it crosses Principale Street. This move will allow you to begin tracing a path back to Campbell's Bay.

For those who want to cycle on the spectacular *final section of the Cycloparc*, begin your outing at Fort Coulonge and head 18 kilometres to Waltham. Sandy beaches, forests, mountain scenery and wildlife will be yours to enjoy until you reach what was once the end of the Push, Pull and Jerk Railway line. Tour around *Waltham* a bit and then head back to where you started, which of course could be Wyman if you somehow mustered up the energy to cycle the entire 72-kilometre PPJ Cycloparc trail.

Covering the Tracks

Over the years, as roads improved and the number of cars and trucks increased, the need for trains to move freight and passengers declined rapidly. Rail lines closed and suddenly, once-busy tracks found grass and weeds growing between their ties. But as Canadians have become increasingly aware of the benefits of staying fit, old railbeds have become pleasant recreational trails, often thanks to the work of the local community. A perfect example is the *New York Central Railway Line* that saw trains rumble through the Ottawa Valley from 1898 to 1957 carrying goods and people from Ottawa to New York. Today, park your car at the old station in Embrun and cycle to Russell, 7.2 kilometres away, on a paved, flat trail that's also great for in-line skating and cross-country skiing.

Another Ontario rail thoroughfare that once was to have stretched from Kingston to Pembroke also had its days numbered. The Canadian Pacific Railway operated trains along the *K & P* or "Kick and Push" route as far as Renfrew from 1913 to the 1960s. Cyclists, hikers, cross-country skiers, and snowmobilers now replace the loco-motives on the 40-kilometre section between Barryvale, off Highway 511, and Snow Road Station, near Highway 509. The scenic trip through forests and beside swamps and picturesque lakes is best cycled on a mountain bike. But don't forget the insect repellent! For more info call 259-2421.

The latest addition to the Eastern Ontario rail-trail scene is the *Cataraqui Trail* that runs 104 kilometres from Smiths Falls to Strathcona, northwest of Kingston. Board a mountain bike to cycle on part of an abandoned Canadian National Railway line that was built in 1879 to link the Ottawa Valley with the Bay of Quinte. Like the other routes, this former rail-corridor's path is wide and the grade slight, so it's basically an easy cycle. Be sure to fit in some R-and-R time at Chaffey's Locks on the Rideau Canal en route. Call 546-4228.

Lost Villages

Start: From Ottawa, travel east on Highway 417 and then south on Highway 138 to Cornwall.
Route: Easy, off-road cycling primarily on a paved route, 34.5 kilometres one way.

> ### Hint
> To allow time for long sightseeing stops, start out very early or begin your excursion part way.

In the early 1950s, Canada and the United States decided to work in concert to provide an improved navigational route to transport cargo to and from Quebec, the Maritimes, and overseas via the Atlantic Ocean, and to produce hydro elec-tricity from the Long Sault Rapids. Five years is what it took to construct the St. Lawrence Seaway, the world's longest inland waterway, that spans the 3,800 kilometres from Anticosti Island to the head of Lake Superior.

On July 1, 1958, an inundation caused the river's shoreline to be redrawn. As the treacherous Long Sault Rapids were tamed and the St. Lawrence Lake born, the villages of Mille Roches, Moulinette, Wales, Dickinson's Landing, Farran's Point and Aultsville, along with 20,000 acres of agricultural land, disappeared under the rising waters. New towns sprang up instead; others were relocated.

The trails offer a visual feast.

To get a sense of the project's impact on the area, begin cycling in *Cornwall*, one of Canada's oldest permanent settlements in the heart of the St. Lawrence Seaway valley. From the Civic Complex on Water Street, proceed west through Lamoureux Park, keeping to the river side of the canal, which once provided the only way to bypass the hazardous rapids.

Go under the *Seaway International Bridge* that links Canada and New York State, and come face to face with the gigantic *R. H. Saunders Generating Station* looming in the distance. Created as a result of the Seaway and Hydro Project, this hydroelectric power dam's capacity of almost 1,000 megawatts makes it one of the largest such plants in Ontario. On the other side of the fast-moving river, the United States makes electricity using the same structure.

From here, the paved trail runs parallel to County Road 2, and soon passes Guindon Park's forest, which is rich with fragile wildflowers and the songs of yellow warblers, northern orioles and red-winged blackbirds. Continue on to Ault Park's *Lost Villages Museum*, a delightful place to stop in the summer months to learn more about the settlements that disappeared when the rapids were silenced and the land flooded. Visit the interpretive centre in the old MacLeod House, and then have a look at other important parts of the St. Lawrence community that had to move because of the seaway's construction. The names say a lot about the disruption—Moulinette Train Station, Zina Hill Barber Shop, Ernie McDonald's Blacksmith Shop, Howard Manson/George Lapierre Grocery Store, and Sandtown Church. Before leaving, explore the museum in the Roxborough Schoolhouse, and then indulge in a cold drink or ice cream.

Further along the path, at about the 14.5-kilometre point, the route connects to the lightly travelled, two-lane, nine-kilometre *Long Sault Parkway* and traverses 11 of the St. Lawrence Islands. Besides very impressive scenery, the area includes three serviced campgrounds, nature trails and formal and informal picnic spots. Don't miss the historic display explaining more about the St. Lawrence Seaway and the hydro project, and expect to see scuba divers out exploring the lost villages, old locks and shipwrecks known to be resting on the river's floor.

Leave the Long Sault Parkway and continue west over a causeway and on towards a bird watcher's paradise six kilometres away. The *Upper Canada Migratory Bird Sanctuary's* swampy marshland was born when the seaway and the hydro project construction caused the water table to rise. Stroll the four nature trails in search of the 150 forest bird species that have been known to call this place home. If your timing is right, perhaps there will be waterfowl feeding here during the fall migration.

To cap off a perfect day of St. Lawrence Seaway exploration, leave the sanctuary and cycle on the five-kilometre gravel pathway to *Upper Canada Village* ($), named the top national/international attraction in 1999. Step back to the 1860s while exploring this fabulous 50–hectare site on the St. Lawrence River. Costumed interpreters and over 40 historic buildings allow visitors to step back in time to learn about life in the 1860s. To contact either the village or bird sanctuary call 1-800-437-2233, or visit www.parks.on.ca.

After a great cycling and sightseeing day, turn around for the cycle back to Cornwall. On the way, reflect on the huge impact the St. Lawrence Seaway and Hydro Project has had on life in this valley, and keep your eyes open for one of the huge ships that ply the river. Each day, about ten vessels now carry commodities such as coal, grain and iron ore up the waterway, compared to the 40 or so that did so in the 1960s. This number is expected to decline even further in the years to come, as the newer container ships are wider and deeper than will fit into the system's 15 locks.

Thousand Islands Parkway

Start: From Ottawa, travel west on Highway 417 and south on Highway 416 to Highway 401. Go west and get off at Exit 696 for Brockville, or Exit 675 for the shorter day trip.
Route: Easy, with some moderate hills along a paved cycling path.

Annually, thousands of Canadian and international visitors travel to Ontario to marvel at the Thousand Islands, which jut out of the mighty St. Lawrence River. Many of the islands located between Brockville and Kingston are privately owned, while others such as Adelaide, Constance, Georgina and Gordon are part of the *St. Lawrence Islands National Park*.

> **Hints**
> Cycle west into the wind first. Pack a swimsuit, and identification if visiting Boldt Castle. If you are not a Canadian or American citizen, bring a valid passport and a United States visa.

This 21-island scenic area offers hours of summertime pleasure for picnickers, swimmers, hikers, scuba divers, and campers who travel to the islands by private boat. Nature lovers without water transportation can enjoy a view of the islands and some of the same outdoor activities at the 38-hectare *Mallorytown Landing* ($), a day-use area 20 kilometres east of Brockville that also serves as the park's mainland headquarters. For information call 923-5261.

As well, a paved path that parallels the Thousand Islands Parkway allows cyclists the freedom to observe the island's palatial homes and rugged shorelines from the saddle of a bicycle rather than from the confines of a car. This route, beginning about ten kilometres west of Brockville, stretches almost to Gananoque. Really ambitious cyclists complete the 74-kilometre return trip in a day. Others start at Brockville (call 1-888-251-7676) and then stay overnight in Gananoque (call 382-3250), to make this a two-day affair. Both vibrant, shoreline cities offer historic sights, live theatre (Brockville—St. Lawrence Stage Company, Gananoque—Thousand Islands Playhouse), riverfront festivals, and excellent dining.

Then there's this third, one-day option that cheats a bit on the cycling (it's about 40 kilometres return), but allows you to fit in a cruise among the Thousand Islands and perhaps a short swim. To give it a try, park at Poole's Resort Lookout Point, about five kilometres east of Rockport, to have a look at the stately summer home and Grenadier Island in the distance. Begin cycling here west, past Rockport, watching for the *Thousand Islands International Bridge*. Opened in 1938, this structure, which is actually three different bridge spans, totals about 13 kilometres in length. As it crosses the St. Lawrence River connecting New York State and Ontario, it touches down on several islands. The famous Skydeck is on Hill Island. It's a bit hilly along this section of the cycling path, so slow and steady does it.

When the route gets to the bridge's traffic interchange, cautiously cross the highway and then rejoin the recreational path again as it goes uphill past the village of Ivy Lea and on to the *Gardens at Landon Bay* ($). Stop here awhile and hike the short Lookout Trail for one of the best views there is of the Thousand Islands. Flower lovers can also enjoy the environmental and theme gardens and the Rosette Pavilion, built especially for the disabled community.

Continue west to *Gray's Beach Parkette*, a small sandy bay that's great for a swim, a picnic and a rest after the long, often uphill ride it took to get this far. Turn around here and retrace your tracks to the *Landon's Bay Bridge*, where perhaps you'll see the flocks of waterfowl that often frequent this area. Along here, and the whole route for that matter, stay alert for great opportunities to photograph the Thousand Islands.

When you reach *Rockport* again, head down into this charming village, which was settled in the late 1700s by the Irish and the Scots. Today it's one of the most popular spots for those wanting to take a trip ($) among the Thousand Islands. One and two-hour sailings are offered on large triple-deck boats, or board a Heritage 1000 Island Cruises vessel (call 659-3151 or 1-888-229-9913) for a stop at *Boldt Castle* ($), on Heart Island. Once there, it won't take you long to realize how much American George Boldt loved his wife Louise.

In 1904, the six-story, 120-room summer home he was having built for her was in the throes of construction when she passed away unexpectedly. Hammers were laid down and saws silenced. For years the castle became the grand home of seagulls and drifters. Today, some parts of the castle are restored to the state they were left in, so it's well worth an hour or so to wander the rooms and grounds, imagining how spectacular the place would have been had it been completed.

When you're cruising back to Rockport, remember that the world-famous Thousand Island Dressing originated in this beautiful part of the world. Legend has it that Boldt was out yachting when his chef discovered that ingredients for George's favourite salad topping were back on shore. He improvised, and the dressing's tangy taste was an instant hit. So much so in fact, that it immediately became a regular part of the menu at Boldt's American hotels. Back on shore, try some on the deck of the *Boathouse Restaurant* (circa 1852) before cycling back about five kilometres to your car.

Wolfe Island

Start: From Ottawa, take Highway 417 West, and Highway 416 South to Kemptville. Go west on Highway 43 and south again on Highway 15 from Smiths Falls to Kingston. Take Highway 2 West across the causeway and watch for signs to the ferry dock.
Route: Travel on relatively flat gravel or paved country roads.

Abandon your car and your cares in Kingston, and head for a day of fabulous cycling on Wolfe Island. Daily, a 55-car ferry takes 20 minutes to reach the largest of the Thousand Islands in the St. Lawrence River. Leave your vehicle at the dock and climb on board (between 6:00 A.M. and midnight) —just you, your bike and a picnic.

> **Hint**
>
> To visit Cape Vincent, bring identification. Non-Canadian or American citizens need a valid passport and a United States visa.

When you reach the island, imagine this pastoral spot being inhabited by the Iroquois many years ago. Today, the place is permanent home to 1,200 people and cottage country for 1,200 more. Many of the residents live in *Marysville*, close to the ferry dock. Named after the village's first postmistress, look for a bakery, restaurants, general stores and a handful of other small businesses in the village.

Starting at the historic town hall, several cycling choices zigzag across the island on well-maintained roads or lightly travelled highways. For me, one of the best R-and-R days happens when I simply head out on an adventure of discovery. I suggest you do this here, for it's hard to get lost on this 34-by-11-kilometre island. If you do, one of the friendly inhabitants is sure to point you on your way again.

From Marysville, paved Highway 96 crosses Wolfe Island horizontally in two directions. Take the shorter western leg of about 5.5 kilometres for a relaxing trip close to the water. At the end, hop the cable ferry to *Simcoe Island*, a stone's throw away, and cycle up the gravel road to photograph the lighthouse. If you take the highway east instead, to the foot of the island, check out the mixed agricultural lands and the smattering of homes that dot the countryside along the 26.5-kilometre route.

If you fancy going to *Cape Vincent*, New York, for a swim and a look at Tibbet's Point Lighthouse, cycle on Highway 95 (6th Concession Road) about 12 kilometres to the Horne's Ferry ($) terminal, and then commence a 10-minute ride to the mainland anytime between 8:00 A.M. and dinner time. Even if you don't want to leave Canada, take this worthwhile cycle to the ferry terminal anyway to watch gigantic ships travel the St. Lawrence Seaway.

No matter which route you choose, when on Wolfe Island keep your eyes peeled for old churches and cemeteries, and hotels or B and Bs in case you decide to stay over. Fishing charters are popular here, and cyclists often come in the spring and fall for migratory bird watching.

After a day away, plan to be out on the Wolfe Island Ferry's deck to see the impressive Kingston skyline, as the vessel cuts a swath back to the mainland, and your car. *Fort Henry* ($) and *Fort Frederick's Martello Tower* (on the grounds of the Royal Military College) stand to the right. The latter houses the history of military education in Canada, while Fort Henry hosts sunset ceremonies, tattoos and other festivities throughout the year. Built between 1832 and 1837, Fort Henry was the replacement for an existing War of 1812 structure that was meant to protect Kingston, the entrance to the Rideau Canal, and the naval dockyard at Fort Frederick.

Note: Another time, why not consider a 35-kilometre getaway to Howe Island. The Pitt's Ferry ($) boards off County Road 2, about 65 kilometres east of Kingston. Take a journey three quarters of the way around the island, close to the shoreline, before crossing the water back to the mainland. Here, you'll find yourself less than five kilometres west of Gananoque, so if you're in the mood take a side trip into this exciting city for a bite, before pedalling back to your car.

EXPLORING ON FOOT

Since I've lived in Ottawa, Eastern Ontario and Western Quebec's varied terrain has allowed me some very special outings in the mountains, beside the water, or through fields of showy wildflowers. Many of the trails I've included here make for a great spring, summer or fall day's outing, and some are sure to beckon you back again come winter so you can see how magical the environment has become.

Here are a few of the best hiking and cross-country spots in Ottawa, Gatineau Park, and Mont Tremblant Park in the Laurentians to get you out in the fresh air at various times of the year. Each explains how to get to the trailhead and a bit about what to expect once you're there. Throughout, key sightseeing spots or landmarks to keep you on the right path are indicated in italics. Parking lot numbers are noted as (P?) where applicable.

When you're deciding which spot to explore, if nothing in this section appeals at the moment, use this book and your imagination to come up with your own idea. For example, many of the "Sightseeing on a Bicycle" excursions lend themselves perfectly to relatively flat cross-country skiing adventures.

Novices should try a short, easy outing the first few times out, or complete only part of one of the more difficult and/or longer trails. To save some time and energy, why not take two cars and leave one at either end, or park part way and begin from there.

Remember to zigzag on steep terrain, especially if you are not feeling confident, and to take it slow at the beginning of the hike so you don't get tuckered out right off the bat. Try to set out early in the day so you'll be back before dark. If you're going alone, it never hurts to let someone know your plans.

Before leaving, get yourself prepared for a day away. Wear sturdy, good-fitting, broken-in footwear, and bring a light daypack to carry lots of water, snacks and/or lunch, and the rest of your stuff. For hiking, consider carrying a walking stick or old cross-country ski pole if the trail is expected to be wet or steep. If cross-country skiing, ditch the sun hat and bug spray, and instead pack wax, scraper, cork, matches, and gaiters to keep your pants dry. In all cases, be prepared for a change in weather.

Just in case you can't find a pit toilet at the beginning of the trail or en route, tuck some tissue into your pack in case you must resort to au natural. In the warm months, bring and use insect repellent.

As well, always be on the lookout for poison ivy, the untouchable that grows as a shrub, vine or small plant with three shiny leaves and clumps of white berries. As the saying goes, "Leaves of three, let them be." Any time you notice an unusual rash, blisters, swelling or itching, remove your contaminated clothing immediately and wash the area with soap and water. Calamine or other medicated lotions may provide relief, but if not, or if your reaction is severe, get to a doctor right away.

Finally—whichever outing you choose, remember that exploring the outdoors on foot is a fabulous way to improve your physical and mental health as you commune with nature.

Ottawa's Greenbelt

Start: From Ottawa, follow the directions below to the numbered parking lots (P?).
Route: Easy, well-maintained trails of variable length in the six separate sectors.

Hints
Go often! Secure a map ($) showing all routes from the Capital InfoCentre, across from Parliament Hill.

Prime Minister Mackenzie King was a visionary—a visionary who realized back in 1937 that Canada needed a beautiful capital city. Jacques Gréber, a French urban planner, was hired, and by 1949 a "green necklace" befitting the nation's capital was in the works to inevitably control its urban sprawl. The result, a 20,000-hectare natural space set aside for research, government institutions, agriculture and conservation, that today offers residents and visitors an open invitation to hike, cross-country ski, snowshoe or bird watch on 100 kilometres of glorious trails.

Starting in the east, the six jewels of the necklace are strung so that the clasps end up on the shore of the Ottawa River. In order, there's Greens Creek, Mer Bleue, Pine Grove Forest, Pinhey Forest, Stony Swamp and Shirleys Bay.

Each of these gems is special, but the *Mer Bleue Conservation Area* tops them all—it's so unique that an international treaty protects it as a wetland. The highlight—a 1.2-kilometre, self-guided walk along the boardwalk—heads off through a hardwood forest and cattail marsh before reaching a peat bog area typical of those found much further north in Canada's boreal forest, around James and Hudson Bay. Visit this area and then venture on a 6.7-kilometre jaunt on the second route nearby. From Ottawa, travel east on Highway 417 to Anderson Road. Go north as far as Ridge Road, and then right to the end to find P22 where both paths begin.

Mer Bleue covers 2,300 hectares. A total of 15 kilometres of its trails are groomed for cross-country skiing. To explore 12.4 kilometres of these paths in a completely different part of the conservation site, drive back along Ridge Road to Anderson and travel north to P19, across from the Natural Resources Canada Geomagnetic Laboratory. Carry some sunflower seeds, because the friendly black-capped chickadees are sure to be flitting about looking for a handout along the well-maintained trails that cut here and there through the woods.

Speaking of birds, when hiking, cross-country skiing or snowshoeing with the family at the *Stony Swamp Conservation Area*, expect to bump into more of the forest's feathered friends looking for a bite to eat along the Jack Pine (P9), or Beaver and Chipmunk (P8) trails. Bring your binoculars, as these paths are a birdwatcher's paradise. Travel west on Highway 417 to Highway 416, and then south to Hunt Club Road. Go west to Moodie Drive and left to the parking lots.

A short distance away, take a one-kilometre stroll to see ruins of the nineteenth-century, stone Flood Lime Kiln. Up until 1906, limestone quarried here on site was heated to such high temperatures that the carbon dioxide burned off and lime was produced. Limited parking is available on the road south of P9.

Elsewhere on the 2,000-hectare Stony Swamp site, recreational paths wind through beautiful natural areas. Some of these leave from P10 on Hunt Club Road, including 11.5 kilometres of the 300-kilometre Rideau Trail that takes avid outdoor enthusiasts on foot or skis from Ottawa to Kingston. To find a pleasant wheelchair-accessible trail, proceed along Hunt Club to Richmond Road. Go right to find the 0.8-kilometre Sarsparilla (P7) trail.

It's the varied landscape that makes the Greenbelt's jewels so interesting. Two forests offer a chance to get lost amidst their wonder. At *Pinhey Forest*, try the keep-fit stations along part of the 5.5-kilometre trail, located by taking Highway 417 West to Woodroffe Avenue and then going south to P13 behind the Nepean Sportsplex. Drive to P14 instead (continue south on Woodroffe and left on Slack Road) to hike or cross-country ski along 3.2 kilometres of trails in an area where sand dunes once existed; poplar and red pines planted to stop erosion 50 years ago tower above today.

At the second forest, *Pine Grove Forest*, hundreds of stately deciduous and coniferous trees provide a delightful destination for summer and winter activities. From downtown Ottawa, take Mackenzie Avenue and go right onto Wellington Street. At Bank Street (Highway 31), go south, and turn left onto Davidson Road. Continue past Conroy Road to P17 to find bird-watching trails and forestry-interpretation routes.

Elsewhere in the 12-square-kilometre Pine Grove Forest, discover 7.4 kilometres of trails, designated cross-country skiing only, from P16 off Bank Street. Continue on Bank past the intersection with Conroy Road and go left on Leitrim Road past Hawthorne Road to locate another six kilometres of paths that start at P18.

The last two sections of Greenbelt land each front the Ottawa River, and both are primarily for cross-country skiing. At the *Greens Creek Conservation Area* in the east, 5.5 kilometres of trails are unique because they consist of many short loops. Travel east on Highway 417 and Highway 174 and exit at Montreal Road. Go east on St. Joseph Boulevard and turn right at Bearbrook Road to P24, where you will find both a toboggan hill and the trailhead. To start exploring the trails in reverse, go south on Bearbrook Road to P23 (Hornets Nest Park).

At the west end of the green necklace, the jewel is the *Shirleys Bay* sector. Travel west on Highway 417 and north on Moodie Drive to Carling Avenue. From P2, ski along a four-kilometre route offering picturesque views of the Ottawa River, or a 6.4-kilometre path that passes the spot where limestone was harvested for the Parliament Buildings. Travel west on Highway 417 to Moodie Drive and go north. Turn left on Corkstown Road to P3 just beyond the National Capital Equestrian Centre.

Rideau Trail

Some people are just not content with spending only a few hours recuperating in the outdoors after a hectic week at the office. For them, hiking, cross-country skiing, or snowshoeing part of the 300-kilometre Rideau Trail may be just the getaway they need. The route, marked with orange isosceles triangles, provides scads of opportunity to be out and about for one day or several. It traverses public and private forests and agricultural tracts, starting at Kingston's Cataraqui Conservation Area and ending at Ottawa's Richmond Landing on the Ottawa River near Victoria Island. Generally, it's more rugged south of Perth. Members of the Rideau Trail Association's Ottawa, Kingston and Perth clubs maintain the trails and organize outings on Saturdays and Sundays throughout the year, either along the Rideau Trail or to other hiking destinations. Their guidebook, available in bookstores or by mail, includes detailed maps and descriptions. In Ottawa call 860-2225, or in Kingston 545-0823, or visit www.ncf.carleton.ca/rta.

Meech Lake Ruins

Start: From Hull, take Highway 5 North to Exit 12 for Old Chelsea. Turn left and continue straight through the village and then right along Meech Lake Road to P11 at O'Brien Beach ($ for parking mid June to Labour Day).
Route: Gentle up and down for an hour.

Back in 1987, Canadians from coast to coast met at the dinner table, in the boardroom and over the back fence to debate the merits of granting Quebec special status as a "distinct society." That year, Prime Minister Brian Mulroney and the provincial premiers also gathered at the stone summer home

> **Hint**
> Bring your bathing suit.

of Thomas "Carbide" Willson, high up on the cliffs above Meech Lake in Gatineau Park, to discuss this and other ideas to reform Canada's constitution.

Unfortunately, viewing this historic meeting place up close is not possible. What is though, are other traces of this man Willson, who spent hours studying chemical fertilizers. Remains of the workplace where he eventually produced calcium carbide are well worth a look.

To get there, take *Trail 36*, beginning near the sign at the back of the O'Brien Beach parking lot, and head up the hill alongside the road. Walk right of the heavy aluminum gate and under the Discovery Trail's canopy of maples, birch and oak in the direction of Herridge Shelter.

Soon you'll encounter an interpretive sign explaining the area's geology. Look for evidence of the destruction that was caused when tons of ice pounded the park in 1998, before you come upon the *wooden footbridge* that divides "big" Meech Lake from Little Meech. Their namesake, Reverend Asa Meech, was a congregational preacher famous around here for his community work. His body rests in the Protestant cemetery down the historical path directly across from the general store in the village of Old Chelsea.

Before long, smell the earth's dampness as you ascend the hill past the lacy ferns. At the *trail's junction* that reports you have hiked one kilometre, go right and begin the climb through the mixed hardwood forest. Soon the route descends to the Willson ruins, on a path that often sees its centre chewed apart by the rain. Tread carefully.

Follow the route around the hairpin curve to an impressive sight kerplunk in the middle of nowhere. The roofless, grey-stone generating station, acid-generating tower and thundering waterfall at the beginning of Meech Creek mark the spot where "Carbide" Willson followed his dreams. Another day, if you cycle or walk the "Parliament Hill Splendour" route, look for his abandoned mill on Victoria Island.

Linger by the falls, soaking up the mystery and beauty of this place, before retracing your steps to the large rocks near the footbridge that make a perfect spot to enjoy a snack and contemplate life. Either later today or another time, spend a few hours swimming at Meech Lake's O'Brien or Blanchet Beaches (four kilometres further past P11), or take a leisurely canoe trip along its five kilometres of sun-dappled water.

A note of warning: Nudists love to swim and sunbathe along the Meech Lake Ruins Trail. I've never seen them—you may!

Skyline Trail

Start: From Hull, travel north on Highway 5 to Exit 12 for Old Chelsea. Turn left and proceed through the village as far as Kingsmere Road. Turn left and continue to P7.
Route: A steep stretch to begin; otherwise rolling hills.

Skyline Trail is one of Gatineau Park's most popular destinations for hikers and cross-country skiers, as the views from the top are picture perfect year-round. To get there, though, means taking a trail that, after its gentle start, begins a long, steady climb. Be patient, don't overdress and take your time on this stretch of shared Trail 30, knowing that once you master this hill, it's basically smooth sailing for the remainder of the hike.

> **Hint**
> Make this a lazy-man's two-hour hike to allow time to absorb the scenery from atop Gatineau Park's magical world.

Rest at the lookout on the right, near the directional sign, to enjoy the Ottawa-Hull cityscape nestled in the valley below. Afterwards, select *Trail 1* to the left towards Keogan Shelter, and continue a few metres up the steep hill until you reach Skyline's *Trail 6* on the right. Take this route and listen for the birds as you traverse forests of maples, oaks and other hardwoods. Some of the biggest red maple leaves I have ever seen dress the trees here in late September and early October.

At Trail 6's *Y intersection*, choose the left fork to save the best for last. The narrow trail wanders up and down over rolling hills past another trail intersection, but keep to Trail 6, which may be wet in places. Use caution. When you reach the *T junction* at the edge of the escarpment, take a fifteen-minute side trip left to the Skyline Slope of the Camp Fortune Ski Hill to savour unobstructed views of the Gatineau River and beyond.

Retrace your steps back to the trail, and before long there is a wonderful spot to enjoy a view of the valley below. Interpretive panels nearby indicate that this part of the trail was built as a work project in the Great Depression of the 1930s, so that all trail visitors could experience these gorgeous panoramas.

Meech Lake Ruins

A bit further along, keep your eyes open for a wonderful, high-backed bench, which offers a perfect place to rest and soak up the marvels of nature. From here you can see the Gatineau River and the village of Old Chelsea in the distance. Remember to stop at this bilingual community's fine restaurants and galleries on your way back to Hull.

Continue along the ridge for more vistas of the countryside until eventually you return to the *loop's beginning*. Retrace your steps to where the path intersects Trail 1. Go left, back to the signpost, and then rejoin Trail 30 and the steep descent back towards the parking lot.

Note: On cross-country skis, the Skyline Trail is rated as intermediate to difficult particularly because of its narrow width and steep hills. The last stretch to the parking lot can be very treacherous, so take your skis off if need be, and walk down beside the ski tracks.

Mont Bleu to Pink Lake

Start: From Hull, take Highway 5 North exiting at St Joseph-Mont Bleu. Follow the signs to Mont Bleu Boulevard and continue through the residential area to the end. Park at P2 at the right rear of the Collège de l'Outaouais ($ on school days).
Route: Moderately steep ups and downs.

> **Hint**
> Take this two-and-one-half-hour hike on a cooler day, as part of the trail is without shade.

Without a doubt, one of the most exquisite natural jewels in Gatineau Park is Pink Lake. Named after a family that settled in the area in the 1800s, this fragile aquatic marvel can easily be reached by car along the Gatineau Parkway. If, however, you want to relieve yourself of some stress and maybe even a little weight, get there my way instead.

Trail 26 begins at the parking lot's back exit, where there's a map. It continues on a dirt path beside the hardwood forest and through wide-open spaces until it reaches *Trail 5*. Go right, staying alert for fast-moving cyclists, along this shared, paved path that's lined with daisies, buttercups, prairie clover and an assortment of other colourful wildflowers on warm summer days.

At the Leamy Creek Pathway intersection, proceed on Trail 5 in the direction of Pink Lake. Not too far along, on the left past the paved intersection, a small wooden post indicates unpaved *Trail 25*, which takes you through a field and up the short, steep hill ahead.

Once on top, the path soon passes a large, swampy area. Search for clues as to why the water drowned all of these hardwoods.

From here to Pink Lake, you'll be greeted by impressive scenery at every bend, as the route winds its way up, up, up between massive, tree-covered cliffs. Watch for a chance to hug the gigantic evergreen. How old do you think it is?

Eventually, the path meets up with *Trail 5* again, which is now a dirt path. Take it left until it intersects *Trail 15*. After a long, wooded section, go left at the *Y intersection* down a very steep hill and on towards the Pink Lake parking lot. Proceed past an old beaver pond, leafy green ferns that line the forest floor, and sumacs that are sure to be deep red come autumn. Now you know what you would have missed if you had driven here instead!

At *Pink Lake*, lookout points with interpretive panels provide information about this unique and beautiful spot. It's an abundance of microscopic algae that creates its incredibly beautiful colour, and a home for a type of fish with an interesting life story.

Some 11,000 to 12,000 years ago, a saltwater sea covered these parts, and the three-spine stickleback thrived in its water. In time, the salt water receded and fresh water took its place. Being the adaptable species that it is, the stickleback lived on to tell this tale to the scientists who research the characteristics of the organisms that inhabit this wondrous place.

Another highlight of the lake is that it is meromictic, which means the water lies layer upon layer. As these never mix, the water near the bottom contains no oxygen. As a result, at depths of four metres or more, any branches, leaves and other objects that fall in don't decompose; instead, they remain preserved forever among the sedimentary deposits that date back 10,000 years.

The footpath makes a circuit around the entire lake, so you can study its beauty more. The adventure you are on, however, leaves the Pink Lake area part way along this route, so take the boardwalk stairway down to the lake and choose between two options to reach this hike's departure point. Go straight ahead and to the left to circle the lake about 60 percent of the way, or go right, through the opening in the fence, to find a path that passes close to the west side and will take you 40 percent along.

This second route soon climbs up and down wooden stairs that afford a panorama of the lake's rich green colour. Listen for the forest's warblers, finches and thrushes, or the loons that love this lake. Stop at the bench along the trail that provides a perfect picnic place before you return to the shore again.

Whichever option you choose, locate a *wide trail* carpeted with red-pine needles, a short distance from the end of the lake. Proceed up this path and past the gate that takes you to the *Gatineau Parkway*. Turn left and walk down alongside this busy roadway, keeping an eye out for a set of the power lines above. Proceed under these, and continue another 50 metres or so until you notice a junction with *Trail 5* on the left. Take this to retrace your steps through the meadow, and then go left on *Trail 26* back to the parking lot. This last stretch leaves you just enough time to ponder who in the world would ever drive to Pink Lake.

Larriault Trail

Start: From downtown Hull, take Laurier Street and Alexandre-Taché Boulevard to the Gatineau Park entrance. Turn right and continue north on the Gatineau and Champlain Parkways to the Larriault Trail parking lot on the left.

Route: Rolling terrain (a few places are steep) makes this a great outing for families with school-aged children.

> **Hint**
> Two to three hours allows time to explore Moorside and Kingswood.

Where else in Canada can you take a delightful stroll through the woods and then stop for afternoon tea on the estate of Canada's longest-serving prime minister? Come along and find out.

The *Larriault Trail* begins where a set of steps ascends the hillside opposite the parking lot's entrance. Notice the out-cropping of the Canadian Shield as the path winds gently up and down through the forest. Not far along, a park bench offers a chance to pause and enjoy a bird's-eye view of the Ottawa Valley from high atop the Eardley Escarpment. Below, fences and trees precisely seam lush, green fields, and roads lead to settlements in the distance.

As you continue along the path through the woods, watch for signs of the ice storm that ravaged parts of Quebec and Eastern Ontario in January 1998. When this natural disaster occurred, there was lots of devastation throughout the park. As well, some Eastern Ontario and Western Quebec residents were without electricity for up to three weeks, as power transformer towers and trees crumpled or broke like spaghetti.

Eventually, you'll come to a very tiny stream. Listen carefully as its softly gurgling waters welcome you to Gatineau Park, a place that draws 1.5 million visitors annually. Further along through the tall forest, a fallen log beside a larger babbling brook provides a great place to stop for a snack.

Go right at the *T intersection*, and descend to the waterfall that William Lyon Mackenzie King, Canada's prime minister from 1921–25, 1926–30 and 1935–48, wrote about in 1948: "The water was coming down in full force, like a bridal veil twisting over stones, taking great leaps. It really was a wonderful sight." This invigorating place is especially dramatic in the spring, when the runoff sends blankets of steam wafting up through the warm, fresh-smelling air.

Retreat up the slope, which can be slippery when wet, and continue straight ahead to find a large rock to rest upon, if need be, after the steep climb. Imagine being here with former British Prime Minister Winston Churchill, who is reputed to have strolled this way with King. The ferns and streams make it a tranquil and beautiful spot to search for signs of aquatic life.

Go through the tunnel under the Champlain Parkway and then immediately right, up to a parking lot. Take the steep, paved trail leading to the Abbey Ruins on King's estate to see some stones from Canada's Parliament Building, which burned in the great Centre Block fire of 1916. Look around awhile, and then follow the path to *Moorside* to enjoy the lush gardens and manicured lawns. Use the ruins named "Window on the Forest" as a prop for great photos before stopping for afternoon tea or a light meal mid May to mid October. Picnicking is discouraged on the estate, so enjoy yours along the forest trail and then indulge in a decadent ice cream cone from the snack bar for dessert.

Take the road beside Moorside and stroll to *Kingswood*, the first place King built in 1903 and his favorite spot to rest and reflect, away from the spotlight of the House of Commons. King began cycling in the Kingsmere Lake area when he was a 26-year-old civil servant working as the editor of the Labour Gazette, the official paper of the Ministry of Labour.

In the years before he was elected to Parliament at age 34, King made his mark as deputy minister of the same government department. Back in those years, he, like other Ottawa-Hull residents, became concerned about the

Moorside at Mackenzie King Estate.

logging that was taking place so close to their homes and Canada's capital. King heard them say, "Why not establish a park here for all Canadians to enjoy?"

It didn't take long to sell him on the idea, so during his fourth term (1935–48) as prime minister of Canada he succeeded in getting Parliament to pass a bill authorizing the first purchase of federal land in Gatineau Park. Personally, over the years, his land accumulation amounted to 231 hectares; all was left to the citizens of Canada when he died at age 75. And over time, the government also increased its land holding, such that today Gatineau Park covers 35,600 hectares.

Circle back to *Moorside* through the colourful expanse of wildflowers, and go right past the tearoom and gardens to find a trail on the right. Walk down it until it joins the *Larriault Trail* once more. Go right here and then left as the route winds through maple and hemlock forests towards man-made *Mulvihill Lake*.

Take the paved path down to the shore and linger awhile, enjoying the sunlight glistening off the water's corrugated surface and the rat-ta-ta-tat of a woodpecker interrupting the silence. Later, walk alongside the Mulvihill Lake parking lot and then cautiously across the Champlain Parkway to your vehicle.

Black Lake and King Mountain

Start: From Hull, travel north on Highway 5 to Exit 12 for Old Chelsea. Turn left, and proceed through the village to Kingsmere Road. Turn left and continue to P7.
Route: Rolling hills and the gentle ascent of King Mountain.

Early each spring, white trillium and yellow and purple wildflowers carpet the forest. Each fall, that same floor boasts shades of red, gold and brown high atop Gatineau Park's Eardley Escarpment. Come along to experience the beauty for yourself on the way to King Mountain's interpretive trail, where you can learn more about the species that thrive upon this rocky ridge.

To get there, begin by taking shared *Trail 30* steeply uphill through the pine and hardwood forest as far as the directional signpost. Stay alert for mountain bikers along the way. After the challenging climb, stop at the lookout for a rest and a view of the special sight unfolding at your feet.

Later, choose *Trail 1* to Keogan Shelter, and stay on it the short distance it takes to reach *Trail 17* on the left. Meander along this path as it travels gently up and down through the woods and over the rocks or logs that provide natural bridges over the babbling brooks.

Further along Trail 17, a signpost directs hikers left to King Mountain. Clamber carefully up the steep rock and find the park bench atop what is known as Sugarloaf. What a reward after the climb—here you are, sitting on top of the world! You'll notice not much grows here, and off in the distance you can see Parliament Hill's Peace Tower.

Continue down the other side of the rock, past wetlands on your left, until you come to a sign that reports that it is 1.5 kilometres to King Mountain. Proceed in this direction and cautiously descend from the trail onto the *Champlain Parkway*. Turn left and continue past the Canadian Shield's amazing strata.

> **Hint**
> Shorten this four-hour outing by either eliminating the King Mountain side trip, or by hiking the King Mountain trail only.

At the *King Mountain Trail parking lot*, stop at a picnic table for a perfect vantage point of Black Lake. Proceed down the steps to the *T intersection*, and go right to begin your climb up the north side of the mountain named King, because it sits on what was once Crown land. Before long, this interpretive trail cuts through majestic eastern hemlocks that grow well here without much sunlight. Further along, more sunshine allows forest-floor vegetation and red and white oaks to flourish.

As the route continues its circle left, on a clear day a spectacular view of the Ottawa River and the Ottawa-Hull cityscape awaits in the distance. Below you can see Lac Des Montagnes and the edge of the Eardley Escarpment.

In spots where the sun's rays bake the mountaintop, fewer oaks share space with sparse grassland. Along the way, perhaps you'll see a red-tailed hawk or turkey vulture employing their metre-wide wing span to soar high above the valley.

In a short while, there's a chance to learn more about the majestic beech and maple trees, before the trail descends steeply to a signpost indicating it's two kilometres to the Kingsmere parking lot. Go right to find some of the prettiest scenery there is en route back to the Champlain Parkway. Cross over and proceed down the informal *"No Bicycles" path*. The scent of pine permeates the tall forest as you make your way to *Trail 8* and a sign indicating that you are now only 1.5 kilometres from P7. Along the route, watch for a natural picnic spot beside a rushing stream.

Continue straight ahead on this wooded path, accompanied by the chirp of the sparrows, chickadees and warblers that love this part of Gatineau Park. Occasionally, there'll be a glimpse of houses built near Kingsmere Road. Eventually, Trail 8 joins *Trail 30* again, and a sign points the way back to P7 and your vehicle.

Ridge Road

Start: From Hull, take Highway 5 North to Exit 12 at Old Chelsea. Turn left and proceed through the village to Kingsmere Road. Turn left and continue to P7.

Route: Some steep stretches; otherwise moderate ups and downs on this six-hour hike.

> **Hint**
>
> See how many new sights you can find when retracing your steps.

Residents and visitors to Eastern Ontario and Western Quebec are continually amazed at the extraordinary beauty of Gatineau Park. It sits high atop the Eardley Escarpment, a 300-metre-high ridge created once erosion had sculpted a fault in the earth's crust about half a million years ago. Today, it's the perfect place to observe the magnificence of the verdant Ottawa River Valley.

After a week when e-mail, voice mail and snail mail has stuck your mind in overdrive, put together some birdseed, water and a picnic and take a hike to the Champlain Lookout to marvel at the view yourself.

Set out up wide *Trail 30* that ascends through a stand of pines and a rich hardwood forest. Your stamina may be put to the test right off the bat on this gradual upward climb, so there's no rush—slow and steady does it until the path levels out. Stop for a break at *Wattsford's Lookout* to the right of the trail junction, and enjoy the panorama that includes Hull, Ottawa, and the Ottawa River. Can you see the flag atop the Peace Tower?

Nearby, a sign points the way to *Trail 1*, the route that goes all the way to your destination. Be aware that because Gatineau Park has a honeycomb of hiking and cross-country skiing trails, several of these intersect this trail. Ignore them all. Instead, continue 3.5 kilometres straight ahead along this easy-to-follow shared path that leads to Keogan Shelter. Stay alert for mountain bikers as the wide path winds its way up and down through the mixed forest past delightful ponds.

When you reach *Keogan Shelter*, about 100 metres off the trail to the right, the place may be abuzz as Gatineau Park adventurers enjoy some R and R and black-capped chickadees flit around looking for a handout. There are picnic tables inside and out of this wooden chalet that serves as a year-round shelter.

Back on *Trail 1*, cross the Fortune Lake Parkway—watch for traffic—on your way through the forest to two other shelters. One called *Shilly Shally*, a short distance along, is a tiny, romantic destination that is a perfect place for lunch or dinner. In the winter, many people cross-country ski along this route under a full moon and enjoy a gourmet feast here before heading back.

Moonlight skiing is popular in Gatineau Park and guaranteed to be an experience long remembered. *Huron Shelter*, a kilometre away, is a spot that can accommodate more winter or summer diners; perhaps you'll see a beaver busy at work nearby.

Trail 1 eventually passes another pond shortly before it comes to the first of two signposts pointing the way to the *Champlain Lookout*. Walk across the gravel and paved parking lots for an awesome view of the Ottawa Valley. Perhaps you'll encounter turkey vultures and hawks wheeling through the sky on the updrafts, adventure lovers hang gliding off the cliffs, or members of the local bicycle club getting ready to whiz back down the Champlain Parkway. This is the turn-around point so pique your senses to experience Ridge Road from a different perspective as you retrace your steps to your vehicle.

Trans Canada Trail

In 1992 someone had a dream—a dream to see a 16,800-kilometre shared trail built clear across the second-largest country in the world. Over the years, thousands of other visionaries have purchased a symbolic metre or two towards making the longest recreational trail in the world a reality. Meanwhile, a million or so community volunteers continued work on creating a way for hikers, cyclists, horseback riders, cross-country skiers and snow-mobilers to enjoy Canada's natural beauty from St. John's to Victoria, and north to Pond Inlet and Iqaluit on Baffin Island. Although the trail is still a work in progress, in September 2000 the pathway's official launch saw 5,000 Canadians finish relaying Pacific, Atlantic and Arctic Ocean water across the nation. At that time, it was mixed in a ceremonial aluminum vessel and taken to the Canadian Museum of Civilization to be displayed for a year.

To gain a true understanding of what the Trans Canada Trail means in the Ottawa-Hull area, cyclists, joggers and even in-line skaters, in some places, can join the recreational trail along the stone-dust Watts Creek Pathway in the western Greenbelt. Next they travel along the paved Ottawa River Pathway and across the Ottawa River by way of the Alexandra Bridge. From here the trail continues on the Voyageurs, Gatineau River, Leamy Lake and Gatineau Park Pathways as far as Mine Road on the edge of Gatineau Park. (To join the Watts Creek Pathway from the south instead, take the regional stone-dust bicycle path that runs through Stittsville into Bells Corners).

Along Mine Road, hikers and cross-county skiers can get in on the action by taking 35 kilometres of the Trans Canada Trail on Trails 5, 15, 30, 1, 4, 32, 36, 50 and 52 through Gatineau Park towards Wakefield. Watch for the white circles with the distinct maple-leaf logo that mark the way.

Eventually the route from eastern Canada will run through Montreal, Ottawa-Hull, Carleton Place, Smiths Falls, Sharbot Lake and Tweed before heading west and into southern and northern Ontario. For more information, call the Ontario Trails Council at 1-877-668-7245.

Note: If you enjoyed an outing along the Trans Canada Trail, why not spend $40 to buy a metre of the route. The names of those that already have appear at the pavilions near Ottawa's Portage Bridge and in Hull's Jacques Cartier Park. Contact the Trans Canada Trail Foundation (1-800-465-3636 or www.tctrail.ca) to find out more about taking part in this worthwhile project, the results of which will be appreciated by generations to come.

Brown Lake, with a Sleepover to Count the Stars

Start: From Hull, take Highway 5 and Highway 105 North. Go through Farm Point and take the second turn left after the IGA store to find P15 and the Gatineau Park International Hostel (formerly Carman Trails Lodge) on Carman Road.
Route: Easy trails.

> **Hint**
> Call ahead to reserve a bunk.

Who could forget going to summer camp as a child? Bunk beds, campfires, sing songs, nature. New and old friends. When you have the urge to relive those fond memories and create some new ones, *Gatineau Park International Hostel* ($), just outside the Gatineau Park boundary, provides the perfect atmosphere.

People come to this get-away-from-it-all spot from around the world, so you never know whom you might meet—photographers, artists and musicians love the place. Part of the International Hostelling System, this property invites both members and non members to rent a bunk and stay a night or two. Call 819-459-3180, or go to www.magma.ca/~carman.

To enjoy your time away, leave any five-star hotel requirements at home, and instead bring a sheet, some gourmet fixings to barbecue, and a desire to hang out with the sunflowers, stars and a roaring fire after a hike to Brown Lake.

Before hitting the well-marked route, grab a map at the trailhead and take the path that heads north of the old barn. Continue through the fields, often resplendent with summery blossoms, until you see Notch Road, *Trail 57*. Once in the forest, you can follow this route to Brown Lake or select *Trail 58*, the High Road, which will take you gently up and down through the rolling hills. Eventually, this path will meet up with *Trail 57* again.

From whichever path you chose, follow the signs to *Brown Lake Cabin* to see a sample of the type of accommodation that is provided year round in Gatineau Park for hikers, cross-country skiers and snowshoe enthusiasts. (Reserve this cabin, which sleeps 16, well in advance). A wood stove adds to its cozy atmosphere, and an outdoor picnic table's perfect for those sunny, spring skiing days, or just lazing about on a summer afternoon. Call 819-827-2020 for more information.

If you follow Trail 57 to the cabin, you will come to a junction with *Trail 52*, where you will see signs for destinations that offer longer treks in the park. In a couple of hours or so, you could be at Lac Philippe, the Lusk Caves or

Picnicking near Brown Lake Cabin.

Herridge Cabin. If you hike in another direction, you will be headed for Wakefield on a section of the Trans Canada Trail. The hostel staff is very knowledgeable about all of these routes so get the details from them before setting out for the day.

From this trail junction, retrace your steps back to Brown Lake Cabin, then follow the signs for Carman Trails via *Trail 57*, which is a flat trail that meanders parallel to Brown Lake's shore. Spend awhile photographing this hidden retreat.

Keep following Trail 57, and get ready to begin a long, slow trek up a steep hill through the mixed forest. A short informal trail on the right takes you to a spot offering panoramic views of the area. Later, continue on the main trail down the hill and then right through the forest and the colourful meadow back to the hostel.

Note: If you're staying for a few days, there's lots of outdoor adventure to be had in the area. Why not try mountain biking on some of the park's challenging trails. Bring your own equipment or rent a bike from the Gatineau Park International Hostel and explore nature's beauty along the Discovery Trail. Another alternative is to rent a canoe at the hostel and have the staff shuttle you to one of the nearby lakes or the picturesque Gatineau River.

When you get home, be sure to make a note on your calendar to return once the snow has blanketed the wildflowers and lush grasslands. The hostel operates as "base-central" for some fabulous cross-country skiing or snow-shoeing on nearby trails, so be there to join in the fun. If you need to rent snowshoes, they have them.

Lusk Caves and Lusk Lake When Camping

Start: From Hull, take Highway 5 and Highway 105 North. Go left on Highway 366 to Ste-Cécile-de-Masham and look for the brown Gatineau Park/covered-bridge sign. Turn left and continue through the park gate ($) past Breton Beach to the Y intersection and the Lac Philippe campground entrance. If you are only coming to hike, take the left fork just before the entrance and drive to the Parent Beach parking lot.
Route: The terrain ranges from easy to difficult on this four-and-a-half-hour hike.

Hint
To go cave exploring, bring a change of clothes (including a long-sleeved shirt and pants), a second pair of shoes, a helmet, and a good flashlight or headlamp.

Ottawa-Hull residents and visitors spend a lot of time in Gatineau Park. They mix and match outings most often in the sector near the village of Old Chelsea, located in the backyard of the nation's capital, because they forget that up the road another 30 minutes or so, cross-country skiing, camping, canoeing, swimming, mountain biking and hiking opportunities abound.

Next time you're feeling city weary, give yourself the gift of some precious time in the Lac Philippe/Lac Taylor area. Slip away and find respite for a few hours, or better still camp a few days at either of the northern sector's campgrounds. Call ahead and reserve a spot at *Lac Philippe*, where there are 280 individual and 5 group sites, or at *Lac Taylor*, which has 33 semi-wilderness tenting spots. Call 819-456-3016.

Hiking to Lusk Lake.

When you're camping, the allure of the beautiful scenery on the way up to Lusk Caves and Lusk Lake makes it well worth the trek some morning before you go for a swim. If you're not able to spend a night in the outdoors, drive up from Ottawa-Hull some day and take this hike anyway. Here are the directions if this is your modus operandi.

To get started, take the path at the back right corner of the *Parent Beach parking lot* up through the pine forest. At the first *signpost*, take the route leading left towards the lake rather than the one pointing to Lusk Caves. A short distance along, you'll come to buildings housing beach amenities. Walk past these and locate a trail that will take you right along *Lac Philippe's shore*.

In time, the trail will end up at *Smith Beach*, a popular spot where the campers spend time on warm summer days. Locate the trail just above the campfire circle and walk up the short path to join *Trail 50*. Take this wide, gravelled, shared route left along the lake and through the forest, until at the end of the water you will see an outlet connecting to Lac Mousseau (Harrington), a hidden spot with no public access.

Close by, a sign indicates that it is one kilometre to the caves, a natural phenomenon that begs exploration. On this stretch you'll be thankful you're wearing sturdy walking shoes or hiking boots as you begin your ascent up *Trail 54's* steep, catch-your-breath slope that's carpeted with an assortment of Canadian Shield outcroppings, logs built into the hillside to counteract erosion, and protruding tree roots. Take your time, knowing that this particular terrain will only continue about 500 metres.

Another *directional sign* soon reports only 500 metres more to your destination. It's here for the first time that a walking stick may come in handy, as the route causes you to scramble over the water on rocks and logs. It's fun— the worst that can happen is wet feet if you miss your target!

Ascend the concrete steps beside the delightful pond and read the interpretative signs posted along the way to the *Lusk Cave's entrance*. Many people over the age of ten or so, who are not alone and have brought proper lighting equipment, climb down the rock slide into the cave's water-filled mouth to have a closer look at this fascinating, dark place.

Locate where you are on the interpretive sign's map, and walk about 50 metres further to find the entrance to the easier of the two cave-exploring routes. Although this section has holes in its ceiling that let light peek in, a good flashlight is a must. Take care when you're walking, as the cave's walls may scrape you as you feel your way through this natural wonder.

Find the entrance to a second route back near the interpretative sign. Again, proceed with caution to the exit about 50 metres away. Throughout the year, the water level along both of the cave's paths varies. Expect to find it at least waist deep in spots.

When you've seen enough, get out of your wet duds and retrace your steps all the way back down to the intersection with *Trail 54*. Continue your walk in a clockwise direction towards Lusk Lake, a little bit of paradise tucked away off the beaten track. As the black diamond sign indicates, this part of the route is considered difficult, as the narrow, rugged path winds up between widely spaced trees that allow sunlight to dance alongside lush green ferns. A babbling brook keeps you company for awhile. Watch your step and be prepared to detour along the edge of several muddy spots if it's spring or a wet summer.

Start watching for a glimpse of Lusk Lake through the trees before it disappears again from sight for awhile. The trail is easy here, so it won't be long until you're at a *T intersection* that announces it's 500 metres up a wide, moderate slope to the *Lusk Lake Cabin*. This is one of seven cabins in the park that provide year-round shelter for an indoor feast (overnight stays are allowed in some of the buildings in the winter as well). Alternatively, munch your lunch at a picnic table overlooking the peaceful lake.

From here, it's back to the T, and then straight ahead on *Trail 54* towards the Lac Philippe campsite. It will be a while before you reach a *gravel road*. Go right here, and stay alert for Taylor Lake camping traffic. A short, paved stretch sees you back at the *main road* in no time. Cross this and take the informal dirt path down through a colourful meadow of delicate wildflowers, until a path leads left. Go a short distance and voilà—your vehicle at last!

Note: If you only have two-and-one-half hours to spare, consider a Lusk Caves circuit only. Follow the directions to the caves and have a look around. Later, hike left along Trail 54, as described above, until you see a trail on your right. Take this and you'll find a pleasant route leading you down to Smith Beach. Go right here ten metres or so, and then take the path left down to the shore of Lac Philippe for the return journey towards your car.

Gatineau Park in Winter

How many capital cities in the world can boast having a 35,600-hectare chunk of land, home to coyotes, black bears, wolves, white-tailed deer, beavers and two hundred species of birds only 20 minutes away by car from where their parliament meets? Ottawa-Hull residents and their visitors recognize how blessed they are once they spend even an hour in Gatineau Park.

In the warm months, this restful pocket is lush and green. Come fall it becomes a kaleidoscope of colour, once nature's magic paintbrush touches the maples, oaks and sumac. Each winter the area is again transformed, this time into a snowy wonderland that entices cross-country skiers, snowshoers and hikers to spend a day with only the scent of pine needles and blue sky for company. Two hundred kilometres of groomed

Cross-country skiing in Gatineau Park.

trails provide routes along the parkways and through the forest for classic cross-country skiers and ski skaters. Many of the trails are the same ones that can be hiked in the summer; others provide a new way to explore this snow-covered wilderness.

Season's passes, purchased in advance, provide unlimited access to the trails, and daily passes are available at the parking lots. As well, Gatineau Park has snowshoeing trails and equipment rentals, and seven shelters scattered throughout the park are welcoming year-round, day-use places. Come winter, eight cabins in the woods have bunks that you can reserve for an overnight stay. What about trying some winter camping in the Lac Philippe area?

To purchase an annual cross-country ski pass or winter-trail map, visit the Gatineau Park Visitor's Centre at 33 Scott Road in Old Chelsea, or go to the Capital Infocentre across from Parliament Hill. To get an update on ski conditions or to make reservations for an overnight stay, call 819-827-2020.

The Other Side of Mont Tremblant

Start: From Hull, take Highway 50 and Highway 148 East to Montebello. Take Highway 323 North to St-Jovite and go left on Highway 117 North, past the village about two kilometres to Montée Ryan. Turn right and follow the brown signs along Duplessis Road. At the T intersection turn left and continue to the park's entrance.
Route: The first hike described has a vertical rise of 220 metres; the others cover flat terrain.

People from Ontario rave about downhill skiing, hiking, mountain biking and relaxing at the Mont Tremblant resorts in the Laurentians. They never talk, however, about the spectacular 1,492-square-kilometre provincial park located around the back of the same mountain. As a result, out-of-province licence plates are rare in these parts.

This well-kept Quebec secret, located about 20 kilometres from the more popular area, is home to cougars, wolverines and even bald eagles. But before deciding how to spend a weekend or week at this wildlife paradise, take three short hikes to get a feel for the place.

> **Hint**
> Bring along a picnic, as there is only a snack bar and convenience store at the park.

The first hike, to *La Roche*, begins at the parking lot 500 metres from the Lac Monroe Service Centre. A slow, steady, uphill climb on a well-maintained trail passes a glorious babbling brook in the canopied forest. Benches here and there allow you to regain some steam before heading onward and upward.

Once at the summit, 2.5 kilometres from the start, you'll realize the panoramic view was well worth every step. In the distance, look for some of Mont Tremblant's north-side ski runs. Below, hiking or mountain-bike explorations through the maple and birch forests, the beach at La Crémaillière, and canoeing or kayaking on Lac Monroe all beckon. All in all, there are four hundred lakes and six rivers to experience within the park. After you cautiously hike back down, get into your vehicle for further discovery of this spectacular territory.

Continue right on the main road about eight kilometres to the *Diable Waterfall* parking lot, and walk less than one kilometre to where hundreds of litres of water tumble over the rocks. Linger awhile and listen to the crashing symphony before heading back towards the Lac Monroe Service Centre.

Continue two kilometres south of this point to the *Lac Chat* parking lot. From here, a one-and-one-half-kilometre nature trail passes along the lake's shore and that of the Diable or Devil's River, a place where hundreds of fishermen make the big catch annually. Soon you'll reach one of the most spectacular valleys of the region on the way to *Lac-aux-Atocas*, a pristine hideaway. Interpretation panels and a do-it-yourself, French-only booklet describe the sights along the loop, that even wanders through a cranberry bog.

After a small taste of Mont Tremblant Park, you may hate to leave. This section of the park alone boasts over 600 campsites, 80 percent of which can be reserved in advance by calling 819-688-2281. If a night in the wilds is not your thing, drive to the resort area, which you were close to when you travelled to the park. There, obtain hotel or B-and-B accommodation in a nearby Laurentian village so you can spend the daylight hours here exploring further.

When you're in the area, stop at the *Lac Monroe Service Centre* to learn more about other hiking opportunities of varying lengths and difficulty. Consider renting a canoe for a paddle on Lac Monroe, an exhilarating excursion down the Diable River through the rapids or some canoe camping. Shuttle transportation is available. For those that prefer mountain biking, why not hire a bicycle for an easy or intermediate cycle on the rough-and-ready trails.

In the winter, 56 kilometres of groomed trails ($) that challenge enthusiasts of differing abilities wind through the woods, making the park a perfect destination for cross-country skiing and snowshoeing. A longer back-country trail, with four overnight shelters and winter-camping spots, attracts those looking for an alternate way to commune with nature once the snow flies.

Note: If you're curious about what the more popular resort side of Mont Tremblant is all about when it comes to hiking in particular, plan to come back another time and give it a try. In total there are eight hiking routes

Lac Chat at Mont Tremblant Park.

ranging from one kilometre to seven in length, and from great-for-the-whole-family terrain to that which will require a bit more effort and conditioning. The footpaths traverse fields of yellow, pink and white flowers, and wind past tumbling waterfalls, babbling brooks and an old log cabin once used by the fire ranger.

To do some hiking at the summit, get to the top the easy way via the gondola ($). From there, it's a 30-minute-or-so walk to enjoy 360-degree views of coffee-table-book beauty, and to learn more about the area at the interpretative stops. The kids may enjoy the longer two-kilometre trek that uses the ski trails to circle White Peak.

If you decide to hike back down to the base of the mountain, be prepared for sore calves tomorrow, as it's usually harder on the leg muscles to walk that direction rather than up if you're not in top condition. Believe me—been there, done that, and it hurts!

In the winter, perhaps you'll want to come back to enjoy some fabulous downhill skiing at this same spot. Details about the hill once the snow has fallen here and at other Laurentian sites are included under "Downhill Skiing."

EXCURSIONS BY CAR

I love late May, once the ravages of another Canadian winter are but history. Once again, the leaves are brilliantly green, the creeks gurgling and the sun shining. What better invitation could there be than this to hop in the car and go rambling through the countryside?

These trips, throughout Eastern Ontario and Western Quebec, are culled from my travels in all compass directions from Ottawa-Hull. Each makes for a full-day adventure—many for a traditional Sunday drive. I like to leave early in the morning so I don't feel rushed.

The adventures are arranged beginning with those on the Ontario side of the Ottawa; the ones on the Quebec side follow. While planning your travels, think about sleeping over part way along, to buy yourself more time to uncover more of a particular area at a more laid-back pace. When you're on the road, watch for the posted speed limits, and remember that in Quebec, right turns are not permitted on a red light in many jurisdictions.

As was suggested earlier, explore this whole book when looking for other day-tripping ideas—the sections "Outdoor Spectacles" and "Discovering More Outdoors" are full of them. Don't stop there though. Think about driving the "Famous Residences and People," or "Thousand Islands Parkway" cycling routes instead.

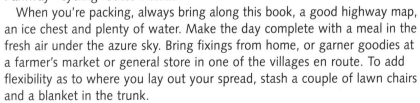

When you're packing, always bring along this book, a good highway map, an ice chest and plenty of water. Make the day complete with a meal in the fresh air under the azure sky. Bring fixings from home, or garner goodies at a farmer's market or general store in one of the villages en route. To add flexibility as to where you lay out your spread, stash a couple of lawn chairs and a blanket in the trunk.

And one last thing before you finalize your plans: try to bring someone to

Fishing at Morris Island Conservation Area.

share the fun and be navigator in chief. After you have this person and any other travelling companions accounted for, are there still unused seat belts in your vehicle that would allow you to share a day in the country with someone else? If you have space for a shut-in or a neighbour's child, I'm sure they'd be grateful.

Finding Food and Flowers

Start: From downtown Ottawa, take Mackenzie Avenue and Colonel By Drive. Go right over the Pretoria Bridge and then left onto Queen Elizabeth Driveway and Prince of Wales Drive as far as the traffic circle.
Route: Mostly travels on county roads.

Hints
Go Saturday if you want to shop at the farmer's market, or in the fall if apple picking is high on your agenda. Bring a cooler and ice packs, and some clothes and gloves to pick your own fruit and vegetables.

Eastern Ontario's long, hot, humid days encourage countless varieties of fruit, vegetables and flora to flourish. It's fun to go for a rural ramble to visit some of the area's exquisite gardens to discover that there's more to life than petunias. Along the way, fill a basket with plump, mouth-watering, farm-fresh produce and specialty foods to savour that day or later on back home.

A perfect place to start enjoying the season's vivid blossoms is at the *Central Experimental Farm's Ornamental Garden*, located alongside Prince of Wales Drive. Depending on the season, wander among the demonstration beds of Explorer roses, peonies, iris, marigolds and snapdragons, or into the colourful sunken garden. In the spring, come to photograph the flowering crab apple trees that flank the roadway, or the Preston lilacs that were developed here in the 1920s.

If you're more interested in starting the day by seeing trees and bushes, drive across the road and through part of the 25-hectare *Dominion Arboretum*, to view some of the 2,400 varieties and species that are either native to Canada, or imports that grow well here.

Later, continue south on Highway 16 (Prince of Wales Drive) past fertile fields and the occasional glimpse of the Rideau River, and turn right onto Bankfield Road. Drive west and go left at 4th Line Road. At *Rideau Pines Farm* (number 5714), pick your own aromatic herbs and vitamin-rich fruits and vegetables, or purchase seasonal produce from their grower's market. For information, call 489-3601.

Further down 4th Line Road, turn right at Pollock Road and go a short distance to buy some cheddar cheese, Swiss-style yogurt or fresh cheese curd (weekends) from the *North Gower Cheese Factory* (number 2515). Proud members of the herd of Brown Swiss cows will be on hand to welcome you.

Watch the cheese-making process through a viewing window inside the store. The factory may be reached at 489-3805.

Back on 4th Line, travel on into the delightful village of *North Gower*. Have a look around this picturesque spot, and on Saturday mornings between mid June and Thanksgiving, follow the crowd right on Roger Stevens Drive to the *Farmer's Market*. Shop for sweet-tasting fruits, seasonal vegetables, scrumptious homemade pizza, and tasty jams, relishes and home-baked pies. For information, call 489-2219.

If you would rather buy organic produce instead, go left on Roger Stevens Drive a short distance to *Cava's Organic Farm*, which can be reached at 820-2929.

Return to 4th Line (County Road 5), and go straight ahead to the Y inter-section. Go left here and on into *Kemptville*. Follow County Road 44 as it jogs left and then right again through this town, which is home to 2,600. Eventually, turn right onto Bedell Road, just past the agricultural fields of Kemptville College.

At the *Evergreen Farm* (number 2170), those who watched PBS's *From a Country Garden* may recognize the hosts, Anstace and Larry Esmonde-White, and the English county garden sometimes seen on the show. Stop for a cup of tea and a cucumber sandwich after admiring the integrally arranged multi-coloured splendour ($). Can you find your way out of the not-to-be-missed, 2.5-metre cedar maze? If so, you're smarter than I! Call 258-5587.

Take the scenic route to Merrickville by continuing down Bedell Road to the T intersection. Detour left into *Oxford Mills* if you want to have a peek inside the Brigadoon Restaurant, with its metre-thick stone walls. Imagine this elegant structure once operating as the village's general store and post office. As well, stop to see the old mill dam and the showy local gardens that add to the allure of this small Ontario village.

Otherwise go right and then left onto County Road 25 until you reach the T intersection. Turn right on Guy Road and continue to Highway 43. Turn right and then left immediately onto Acton's Corners Road. Drive awhile and then follow the road as it curves left onto River Road. The Rideau Canal and soon the *Burritt's Rapids Lock Station* will be on your right. Have a look at the locks and then notice the exquisite stone houses built by the Rideau Canal's stone masons as you head back to Highway 43.

Go right here and a short few kilometres into the historic village of *Merrickville*, often called the jewel of the Rideau. Go left on St. Lawrence Street to find *Mrs. McGarrigle's Fine Food Shop* (number 311), a must-stop shop for award-winning homemade mustards. Add a bottle to your picnic basket and ask for the recipe for chicken with honey tarragon mustard sauce. Use the Canadian Maple variety to make a dish sure to be a hit at your next dinner party.

Retrace your route back down St. Lawrence and Mill Street and cross the canal. Are there any boats passing through the locks? If so, it's worth a short stop to see the historical locking process. Soon, at the junction with *Highway 43*, turn left and watch for the signs to the 3,600-tree *Kilmarnock Orchard* at 1182 Kilmarnock Road. In season, climb a ladder to pick your own juicy, red apples on this beautiful island, or purchase some to take with you from their store. The orchard may be reached at 283-4422.

Get back on Highway 43 and drive on into *Smiths Falls*. Rumour has it that *Hershey's* has scrumptious goodies from the sixth food group that are just waiting to be added to your shopping. Savour the rich chocolate aroma as you tour the factory. Perhaps, at the plant located just off the highway, Oh Henry or Reese's Cups will be moving along the production line. Call the factory at 283-3300.

Travel through Smiths Falls on Highway 43. Turn left at the hospital and continue on to *Perth*. Stroll the streets of this heritage spot, decked out with colourful hanging baskets and eye-appealing planter boxes. Drop by *Stewart Park*, nestled beside the Tay River in the centre of town, to enjoy the floral displays and manicured lawns. This may be the idyllic picnic spot you've been searching for.

When heading out of town along Highway 43 (Wilson Street), detour left on Sunset Boulevard a short way to check out the unique, hands-on *Garden for the Blind* on the grounds of the Lanark County Administration Building. The splashing fountain and 14 waist-high planter boxes filled with vegetation combine to make this a touching, tasting, smelling, listening kind of place. Later, continue to Highway 7 and turn left and then right onto Highway 511 towards Lanark.

Follow the traffic along this road to the very popular *Balderson Cheese Store*. Although cheese is no longer made at this location, a huge selection can be purchased. Pick some up to go with the pie you'll want to make with the apples you've harvested. Do you have room for a double-decker ice cream cone?

Drive slowly as you're leaving the store to see if there is a sign in front of the farm next door announcing farm-fresh eggs for sale. If there is, stop for some before continuing a short way further to a second apple stop, the *Balderson Orchards*. From mid August on, visitors can pick their own great-tasting Lobo, MacIntosh or Courtland apples, or purchase fruit or apple cider at this ten-acre, 1,500-tree orchard. For more information call 259-9153.

You know what they say—always save the best for last. Before the return journey to Ottawa, here's one last chance to sample more delectable chocolate. Pop into *Village Treats* in Lanark, where nothing but the best has been created for over 20 years. Try some irresistible melt-in-your-mouth northern-nugget, butter-crunch or orange-cream goodies—I doubt you'll be disappointed! The phone number is 259-3029.

By now your stomach should be satisfied, your cooler full and you will have seen some beautiful gardens. The fastest way back to Ottawa is to retrace your route in Lanark to find County Road 12. Go left along this road until it becomes County Road 15 and then eventually intersects with Highway 7. Turn left, knowing that you are now less than an hour from Ottawa. It is Highway 417 East that will eventually take you towards where this outing began. Exit at Metcalfe Street and continue to Parliament Hill. Go right onto Wellington Street and then left on Sussex Drive.

Gathering Red and Gold

Start: From Ottawa, travel west on Highway 417 and Highway 7 to Perth.
Route: Travel on some tranquil back roads makes this a fabulous outing, especially in late September or the first half of October when the colours are at their peak.

Each autumn, thousands of Canadian and international visitors converge on certain parts of Eastern Ontario and Western Quebec to see the changing of the colours. And what a sight it is, as the landscape becomes a stunning patchwork of vibrant hues, with some trees so brilliantly gold that you expect to see a puddle of the real stuff on the ground below. In contrast, many other maples stand regally clothed in red, their leaves looking like copies of the one that appears on the Canadian flag.

> **Hint**
> Bring a phone book or textbook to press your treasures as you go.

Why not gather some of these fall souvenirs to use as decorations on a Thanksgiving table, or as treasured gifts to tuck inside a letter mailed to a friend.

Begin by driving around *Perth* to admire the magnificent maples that grace the yards of many of the stone heritage homes. The red-maple's leaves will be red, whereas any sugar maples will be sporting flaming orange come fall. Stop on Gore Street to have a look at the beginning of the Tay Canal, which was built in 1834 to link the town with the Rideau Canal. You're sure to come across the Tay River in your travels today.

Continue on Gore Street south to *County Road 10*. Go right about five kilometres to find a small, green arrow pointing the way to *Glen Tay*. Go right and expect that for the next short while, the route will travel off the beaten track through some serene countryside. Stay alert for signs.

Turn left onto *Christie Lake Road* (County Road 6) and go a short distance to locate the narrow dirt *Bowes Side Road*. Turn left and meander through the picturesque back country to an antique Quaker filling station and remnants of the Bowes Mill on the Tay River. Stop to take a photo of your navigator filling your car's tank at the old gas pump.

Turn right onto Upper Scotch Line Road, and further along, right again onto Noonan Side Road, where you'll find the river accompanying you part of the way as the road winds along to the Menzies Munro Side Road. Go right here and you will soon find yourself back at Christie Lake Road again.

Turn left and watch for a road to *Christie Lake's* north shore. Take this to the top of the hill for a panoramic view of the forest, ablaze with gold, red, and brown. Make a U-turn and return to the Christie Lake Road (becomes Althorpe Road) and continue to the *County Road 36 junction*.

Detour left about a kilometre if you want to stretch your legs on a two-kilometre guided nature walk. At *Bluebird Acres* ($), a 120-hectare homestead farm, hummingbirds, butterflies, trout, herons, white-tail deer and Sandy the sand crane are either full-time residents or guests that stop by each year. Disabled visitors can view the varied habitat from inside a four-wheel drive. Call 273-5449.

If you decide to bypass this stop, turn right at the intersection and no matter what keep following the road to *Maberly*, while experiencing breathtaking views of beautiful lakes and splashes of colour cascading down the hillsides.

Cross busy Highway 7 and go through the village of Maberly. After about 13 kilometres, watch carefully for the small road sign on the left that marks *Robertsville Road*. Get your leaf-pressing book ready to gather some real beauties along this awesome roller-coaster-type road that winds through a mixed forest.

Eventually this road reaches the Highway 509 junction and more striking views of the fall foliage. Turn right here and pass through *Mississippi Station*. Stop along the way to enjoy the rushing water before heading for *Snow Road Station*. Turn right at the church and go on into *Elphin* and wondrous scenes of the forest, awash with the fashionable shades of autumn.

Drive left onto McDonalds Corners Road (County Road 12) and continue into the village of the same name. Watch for signs to *Wheeler's Pancake House* (Concession Road 9), a great destination at which to learn more about the maple tree and maple-syrup production, and to enjoy a nature walk and some delicious Canadian maple syrup. You can reach the pancake house at 278-2788, or at www.wheelersmaple.com.

Leave Wheeler's, and while retracing your route back to County Road 12, look behind the 1868 one-room schoolhouse for the seven-circle, 500-plant *Living Willow Labryinth*. Take the half-kilometre meditative walk and you'll find a silver thyme plant in its centre; this is a gift from His Royal Highness Prince Charles.

When back on County Road 12, turn right and continue alongside pastoral agricultural fields and over the Clyde River into *Lanark*. Proceed through the village until County Road 12 meets County Road 15. Follow this through the countryside until it reaches *Highway 7*. Go left and continue on this roadway and Highway 417 East back to Ottawa.

When home, keep your leaf collection stashed as is until you're ready to do more permanent pressing. To do this, turn an iron on low. Fold some waxed paper, with the wax on the inside, and place the leaf in the centre. Encase this in a tea towel to protect your iron and ironing board, and press the leaf gently for a couple of minutes. Alternatively, use a laminating machine to preserve the leaves forever.

Note: Spectacular views of the fall foliage can be found throughout Eastern Ontario and Western Quebec, particularly where there are plenty of maples. In Gatineau Park, close to Ottawa-Hull, hike or take the chair lift to the top of Camp Fortune (call 819-827-1717), drive to the Champlain Lookout at the north end of the Gatineau and Champlain Parkways, or call the park's visitor centre, at 819-827-2020, for other ideas.

Labyrinths

Today, more people than ever are recognizing the need to balance the physical, mental and spiritual sides of their lives. They do this regularly when hiking beside the water, skiing down snow-crested mountains, or wandering a garden path lined with dainty purple violets and white daisies. Now labyrinths, which invite the spirit to take a peaceful journey, are also springing up everywhere across North America. To experience an entirely different kind of exploration on foot, follow the willow-lined path at McDonalds Corners. Another time, take a 1.2-kilometre meditative walk along the narrow, winding, interconnecting stone pathways of the 13-metre-wide circle on the grounds of Ottawa's Bells Corner United Church. Visit this intriguing spot, which is fashioned after the intricate structure that was laid in 1220 in the floor of the Chartrés Cathedral in France, to commune with your soul. From Ottawa, take Highway 417 West and exit at Moodie Drive. Go south past Robertson Road and look for the church on the left.

Roaming the Ottawa Valley

Start: From Ottawa, travel west on Highway 417 and Highway 17 to Arnprior.
Route: Uses county and secondary roads as much as possible.

It seems when you circle the Ottawa Valley that there are as many stately trees reaching for the sky as there are sheaves of wheat waving in the breeze in all of Alberta. More than half of the Ottawa Valley is water and

Hints

This one-day trip is chock full of things to see and do, so before leaving home, make choices about where to spend your time. Bring a jacket or long-sleeved shirt for cave exploring. Consider an overnight at a B and B (call Ottawa Valley Tourist Association at 1-800-757-6580), or stay in a teepee at the Anishinabe Experience to gain more exploration time.

wilderness, a wilderness that has supported lumbering for centuries. Today, although its role is less prominent, evidence of its impact on the area appears often.

Arnprior, situated at the crossroads of the Ottawa and Madawaska Rivers, about 65 kilometres west of Ottawa, was once one of the valley's bustling lumbering towns. Take the first highway exit into this town of 7,500. Cross the Madawaska River, and you'll be confronted with the specu-lator red limestone building that housed the post office back in 1899; today, go inside for a glimpse of the area's past. Turn right here onto John Street to find a peaceful neighbourhood whose streets are lined with gracious stone churches and grand brick homes built at the turn of the century.

Drive left on Ottawa Street, and proceed to its end to find *Gillies Grove*, an open-air sanctuary that boasts white pines more than 175 years old, the largest basswood tree in Canada, and red-shouldered hawks, which are considered endangered. Several paths wind under the forest's canopy, which filters the rays of sunlight shining on the footpath below. Stroll any of them or take the trail to the right, and in ten minutes you'll see panoramic views of the Ottawa River outside the former home of a McLaughlin Brothers lumber baron (now operated as the Galilee Centre). Notice the tree out front planted by His Royal Highness Prince Edward in 1860.

Retrace your path through the forest, and drive back to the museum. Turn right here onto Madawaksa Street and go straight until the directional signs read County Road 1 or River Road. Motor onwards to experience head-turning views of *Lac des Chats* (Lake of Cats) once the Ottawa River widens. Here and there, patches of dense forest dominate the landscape.

When you get to *Sandpoint*, watch carefully for signs to the Arnprior Golf Course. Turn left here and climb the hill up out of the river valley to find a gravel road that will take you to a T intersection. Make a dogleg right and then left on McLean Drive to reach Highway 17.

Cross this busy thoroughfare and join Highway 508 in the direction of Calabogie to begin making a "square" through the heart of the Ottawa Valley. If it's August and a certain farmer has decided to plant a showy display again this year, "wow!" is the only word to describe what is guaranteed to be both a surprise and one of the most impressive fields you'll ever see during a Canadian summer. A few clues: big, yellow and gorgeous. What a scene to enhance your memories of this part of Eastern Ontario!

Snap a few photos for your album, and then it's on, via a very picturesque

Sunflowers brighten the Ottawa Valley.

route, into the heart of *Burnstown*, one of my favourite poking-around spots. It's the kind of place that if you blink you'll miss it. When you're there, go right to have a quick peek at the gorgeous route the Madawaska River has gouged out of the landscape, and then park in this historic logging village to do some antique hunting and gallery and gift-shop browsing. Include a stop at the café.

Continue along Highway 508 through Springtown, past Calabogie, to locate *Ferguson Lake Road* on the right. Turn here and drive along this back-country road as it snakes its way through the towering woods. At the end of the line, make a side trip left up *Kennelly Mountain Road*. Anytime of year, there are wondrous views of the verdant valley from a short way up—coloured-leaf fans will be especially rewarded in the fall.

Retrace your route down the mountain and go straight ahead this time to catch a glimpse of the region's Irish heritage at *Mount St. Patrick*. Visit the Holy Well, left just past the cemetery, which was established in 1866 by a priest from Limerick, Ireland, on the shores of Constance Creek. On the last Sunday in September, perhaps there'll be a fall supper and bazaar to attend at St. Patrick's Church. When you're driving around, picture how regal the log buildings scattered about this part of the Ottawa Valley must have been in their prime.

Head backwards now for a short stretch as far as the St. Patrick Road/Flat Road junction. Go right here on Flat Road and proceed north past Highway 132 and along the scenic milk run that skirts ditches resplendent with goldenrod and Queen Anne's lace, and dots on the map called Dacre, Balaclava, Scotch Bush, and Hyndford.

Before long, begin watching for the small sign at Fourth Chute Road that indicates the way to the prehistoric *Bonnechere Caves*. Go right to take a 45-minute guided tour ($) 30 metres below into ten-degree temperatures to see remnants of the tropical sea that covered this area about 500 million years ago. Watch stalactites being made, drop by drop, in the limestone cave, and marvel at the pillars of rock created when the Bonnechere River thundered through. If it's a fall visit, expect to see hundreds of bats hibernating under the cave's lofty roof. At any time before leaving, take a short walk to see the rushing waters of the fourth chute. For information call 628-2283, or 1-800-469-2283.

Retreat back to the main road and then go right on into *Eganville*, situated at the fifth chute on the Bonnechere River. Drive over the bridge to see the colourful mural depicting the significance of the river to this community. Turn right at the traffic light and park at the lot adjacent to the tourist information centre. Invite the family to take a walk over the footbridge to Centennial Park for a short kids kind of break. Later, take a quick drive around a village that has been essentially rebuilt since a devastating fire swept through the place in 1911.

If you are planning to spend time at the *Anishinabe Experience* ($), turn left in Eganville onto Highway 60 West (Bonnechere West) and drive towards Golden Lake and the home of the Pikwakanagan First Nation's people. Take the Reserve Road and turn left at the sign of the bear, the community's adopted totem animal, to find a cultural centre where there may be opportunities to make bannock and a craft, or to taste some native cuisine. Shop at the craft store for local Algonquin arts and crafts, and plan to return for their mid-August Pow Wow. Book ahead to stay over in a teepee under the twinkling stars by phoning 625-2519 or 1-800-897-0235, or by visiting www.anishexp.com.

Otherwise, from Eganville take Highway 60 (Bonnechere East) towards Kellys Corner. Follow the road as it cuts cross country through the flag-lined streets of Douglas and then on into *Renfrew*, a place that was first settled in the early 1800s when workers arrived to begin cutting timber. Early nineteenth-century mansions, where lumber barons once lived, give one a hint of this community's roots. If you're in Renfrew in mid July, take in the colourful Lumber Baron Festival (call 432-5131) honouring the town's founders. Otherwise, settle for a walk over one of the last two swinging bridges in Ontario before beginning the 100-kilometre journey back to Ottawa on Highway 17 and Highway 417 East.

To reach the bridge, go up the hill and over the Bonnechere River, and shortly before you reach the centre of the town take the first road on the left and proceed one block to the end of Raglan Street. Park near the dead-end sign.

Murals Extraordinaire

If you enjoyed the beautiful mural in Eganville, I hope this masterpiece just whetted your appetite for what I consider to be the best outdoor art display in the Ottawa Valley—in *Athens*. Someday, you must drive there to see the history of this thriving village painting the town beautiful, whether it's with the B&W train pulling into the station or the image of a summer band concert at the village's bandshell (circa 1925). At last count, there were 12 gigantic, true-to-life canvases making this place picture perfect. You can call 924-2044 for more information.

While you're in the neighbourhood, plan to see the beautiful *Old Stone Mill Museum National Historic Site* down the road in Delta. Built in 1810, the Old Stone Mill is the oldest surviving automatic stone grist mill in Ontario. It's currently undergoing a preservation and restoration project (to be completed in 2002), so right now you can only enjoy the outside. In the interim, learn more about its history at the museum, which may be reached at 928-2584, or www.rideau-info.com/delta/restoration.html.

As well, consider a stop in Forfar at the *Forfar Dairy*, where cheese has been made the traditional way for over 130 years. Shop for carefully aged cheddar and goat's milk or other unique specialty products. The phone number is 272-2107. From Ottawa one of the quickest ways to get there and back is to take Highway 417 West and Highway 416 and Highway 16 South to Kemptville. Go right on Highway 43 to

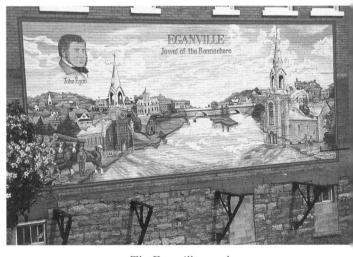

The Eganville mural

Smiths Falls and then south on Highway 29 to Forthton. Go right on Highway 42 to Athens, Delta and Forfar before turning right at Crosby for the return journey on Highway 15 as far as Smiths Falls. From there, retrace your route back to Ottawa.

It's All About Conservation

Start: From Ottawa, take Highway 417 and Highway 17 West to County Road 49 for Carp.
Route: Primarily travels county roads. Some nature trails at Morris Island are wheelchair accessible.

Hint
Select items to bring from the following list: fishing rod, canoe, watercolours or oil paints, binoculars, walking shoes, cross-country skis or snowshoes, or a camera.

According to Webster, "conservation" means controlled use and protection of natural resources. For my sake and yours, and that of future generations, I'm glad a group called Mississippi Valley Conservation exists. They are a community-based environmental organization funded primarily from municipal levies and self-generated revenues. Once in a while, the provincial government also coughs up something for the kitty to assist them in managing the 4,450-square-kilometre Mississippi River watershed.

I would be remiss if I did not tell you about two extra-special jewels within the territory that the conservation body looks after. If you leave at a decent hour and budget your time accordingly, you can enjoy them both within a day.

To really get in the mood for a great day in the natural world, take the scenic route to Morris Island. To do this, turn right off Highway 17 onto County Road 49 (Exit 155). After a short drive through corn country, go left on County Road 5 and on into *Carp*, home of the famous Diefenbunker, a great Saturday-morning farmer's market, and the Garlic Festival of Eastern Ontario each August. Continue through the village and get prepared for the sweet smells of the country and beautiful valley vistas as you drive along to the T intersection.

Turn left here onto the Galetta Side Road (County Road 22), and keep your eyes peeled on the right for the conservation area sign at Loggers Way. Turn here and follow the signs to *Morris Island Conservation Area*. Whichever items you brought, get them out and start using them within this 70-hectare site. Paint a scene that will remind you forever of this stunning hideaway. Hike the well-marked trail network (always stay alert for poison ivy—leaves of three, let them be). Catch a bass, perch or pike along the causeway. Canoe in the tranquil bays of the Ottawa River. Do some birding. Glide through the mixed forest on the snow blanketing the frozen earth. And make sure to leave a donation so others can also revel at the magnificence of this gem. For information, call 259-2421.

When you've seen enough, return to Galetta Road and turn right. Continue ahead and cross Highway 17. Proceed on County Road 22 to the County Road 20 junction. Go left here and on into *Pakenham*. Watch for the five-

Pakenham Bridge

span stone bridge, the only one of its kind in North America. Go left and drive over it to find a spot to get the best photos of the Mississippi River rushing through.

Retrace your route over the bridge and continue left down County Roads 20 and 29 to the large sign for the *Mill of Kintail Conservation Area*. Turn right here and follow the road. Plan to spend two to three hours hiking, cross-country skiing or snowshoeing trails that each take from 20 minutes to an hour to complete. In season, don't leave this 62-hectare site without seeing the museum, cloister on the hill and pioneer cabin, or attending the special educational events or exhibits that take place here often. As well, allow time for a picnic, and for the kids to have a slide at the play structure before the gates close at 4:30 P.M. in the warm weather. Call 256-3610 or visit www.mvc.on.ca.

Later, go back out to County Road 29 and turn right. Go left at *Almonte* Street into one of the most charming Ontario towns there is. Get out of the car and have a look at the Mississippi River roaring past the old woolen mill. If it's not too late in the day, have a look at the Mississippi Textile Museum, the Naismith Museum (inventor of basketball), or at some of the gifts shops or galleries that add to Almonte's appeal.

When you're done, follow the main road through town and along County Road 49 to Highway 417. Follow the signs to get back to Ottawa in about

30 minutes after a day away that will make you appreciate why conservation sites are so critical to life in our modern world.

Note: Another Mississippi Valley Conservation Area well worth visiting is the Purdon Conservation Area. Read about seeing 16,000 orchids in "Flowers, Flowers, Flowers." As well, "Covering the Tracks" explains more about cycling the K & P Trail.

Exploring the Rideau Canal from Ottawa to Westport

Start: From downtown Ottawa, take Murray Street and then Dalhousie Street into the heart of the Byward Market. Park in the York Street area.
Route: Goes from the first set of locks on the Ottawa River to the Rideau Canal's summit at the Upper Rideau Lakes. Locking season is mid May to mid October.

Hints

This is day one of a two-day outing. It also makes a wonderful day trip if that's all the time you have. Start out early and bring a cooler.

When Lieutenant-Colonel John By and the Royal Engineers built the Rideau Canal, little did they know what pleasure this engineering marvel would bring to so many over 165 years later. After the British fought the Americans in the War of 1812, By's mandate was to build a military supply route over the 202 kilometres needed to link the St. Lawrence and Ottawa Rivers. Thousands of Irish and French Canadian workers died over the six years it took to complete this historic Ontario treasure, the oldest regularly operating canal in North America.

To have your first look at their fastidious work, take a walk from Ottawa's *Byward Market* towards the Château Laurier on Wellington Street. From atop the Plaza Bridge you can see the eight locks that move boats 24 metres from the Ottawa River to the top in about an hour and a half. Go down the stairs for a closer look and to pick up a detailed map of the Rideau Canal. History buffs should visit the *Bytown Museum* in the old Commissariat Building ($) to learn more about Colonel By and his influence on the history of Ottawa.

On the way back to your vehicle, stop in the market to pick up some fresh fruits and vegetables, cheese, cold cuts and bread for a picnic. Nowhere in this bilingual city is the switch between French and English so fluid, or the city more vibrant. This was once the centre of commercial activity, where store owners lived above their shops, and hotels and taverns catered to boisterous lumbermen, mill hands and Rideau Canal labourers. Plan to come back another time to enjoy the historic cobblestone courtyards, an evening's entertainment or a pint at the Château Lafayette, which has served beer since 1859.

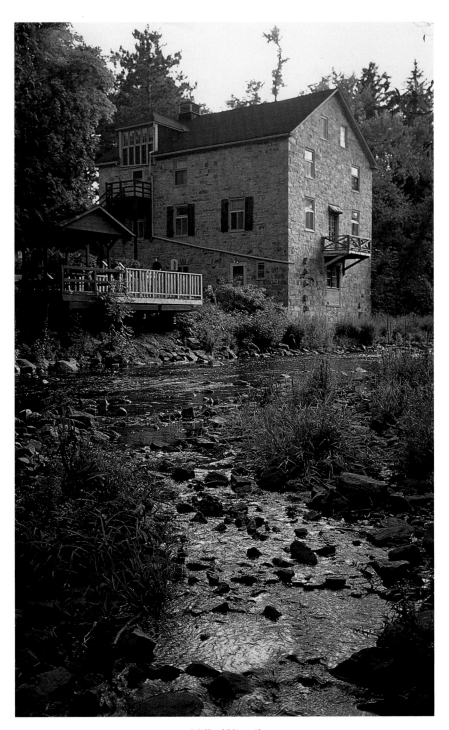

Mill of Kintail

Little Meech Lake

The Enchanted Gardens

Picknicking at Major's Hill Park.

Morris Island Conservation Area

Ottawa's Winterlude

Gendron Bridge

Hikers rest along the Trans Canada Trail.

Once back in your vehicle, head down Colonel By Drive alongside the canal. Picture this artificial route being carved by pick and shovel once By decided there was no way that vessels would be able to navigate the treacherous Hog's Back and Rideau Falls.

Soon you'll pass *Dows Lake*, a great swamp that extended as far as the Ottawa River before it was dammed, and the *Hartwells and Hog's Back Locks*. The former was once a busy maintenance depot, with the square lockmaster's house a defensible stone structure. The locks at both of these stations are operated manually, as are the majority along the canal. A boat needs three to five days to make the Ottawa–Kingston journey through locks that are about 41 metres long and 10 metres wide.

Turn left at Hog's Back Road and right onto Riverside Drive (County Road 19). Eventually you'll pass the Ottawa International Airport. Between here and Westport, there are ten lock stations. Because there isn't time in a day to enjoy them all, I have selected my favourites.

Drive past several residential communities, and watch for the sign telling you to turn immediately right to the *Long Island Lock Station*. Basically, all that remains of what was once a thriving settlement is three locks that climb about seven metres.

Go back to the main road, and then right, until you come to the road that travels over Long Island and the Rideau River into Manotick. Seek out *Watson's Grist Mill*, located on the backwaters of the Rideau River on the left after you're over the second bridge. This stone beauty, the subject of many oil and watercolour paintings, is the last building of an industrial hub that stood here in the 1860s. Take a tour of the site; at certain times, you may see flour being ground. For information, call 692-2500, or check out www.watsonsmill.com.

Continue through Manotick turning left onto its Main Street (County Road 13). Further along, go right at the T junction and then drive slowly through the hamlet of Kars. Soon the Baxter Conservation Area will appear on the left. Occupying about 70 hectares of flood plain along the Rideau, it's open year-round for bird watching, nature hiking, or cross-country skiing, in season.

Continue until the junction with County Road 5 for Merrickville. Turn left and pass Rideau River Provincial Park, which offers 186 campsites ($), beaches, boat launches and opportunities for migratory-bird watching, fishing, and hiking nearby. Call 258-2740 or 836-1237.

At the Y intersection, take the road towards Kemptville. Once over the bridge, turn right onto River Road. At the T intersection, continue on River Road to the *Burritt's Rapids Lock Station* to have a look at what Colonel By's crew built in the early 1800s. Spend an hour and a half walking the Tip-to-Tip Trail if you want to stretch your legs in a beautiful setting.

Once back in your car, go a short distance and turn right into the village itself to see old stone houses and the wonderful general store on the spot

(Following page) Watson's Grist Mill at Manotick.

where the settlement sprang up in 1793. It is said that Colonel Stephen Burritt had been rafting down the Rideau looking for a place to homestead when he came upon the rapids and a perfect spot for a mill. The rest is history.

Back on River Road again, drive right past some of the magnificent homes built by the Rideau Canal stone masons. At the Highway 43 junction, turn right to get to *Merrickville*. This "jewel of the Rideau," as it is often called, was established in 1794 when American William Merrick built a sawmill near the river's waterfall.

Take a stroll around town to see the old mill buildings, historic homes, and the largest blockhouse on the canal, which now contains bayonets, musket balls and a variety of household artifacts from eras past. At one time, Merrickville was considered to be a strategic military site in case of war with the United States. Notice the rifle slits that Colonel By and his crew cut into the thick walls of this 1832 military fortress to protect the lock station. Fortunately, they were never used.

If you want to spend some time on the Rideau River spotting waterfowl, opt for a 45-minute boat ride ($) to the bird sanctuary, or rent a canoe from the Canadian Recreational Canoeing Association, at 269-2910 or 1-888-252-6292. For a longer journey, hire a cruiser at the marina to experience the pleasure of boating through the locks. The phone number is 269-4969.

To explore more of the Rideau Canal, drive over the canal on Mill Street. Perhaps the swing bridge will be letting boats through this busy, three-chamber lock station. Turn left at Highway 43 and head for *Smiths Falls*, once Grand Central Station here on the Rideau. Go into town and turn left on Main Street and left again on Beckwith Street to locate the *Rideau Canal Museum* ($). Visit during locking season, and then take a short walk to see the hydraulically operated combined lock that has replaced the original three chambers.

Smiths Falls is the decision point. If you are making this a one-day outing, head back to Ottawa on County Roads 4 and 6 through North Gower. Go over the Rideau Canal onto County Road 19 and head left back into downtown Ottawa.

Those making this a two-day excursion should drive across the river beside the lock station, and turn right onto Highway 15 (Lombard Street). As you continue southwest, stop at the villages of Lombardy, Portland (on Big Rideau Lake) and Crosby if you want. Otherwise, continue and go right onto Highway 42 and proceed through Newboro to *Westport* for a night at a B and B, inn or campground in this charming village in the heart of the Rideau Lakes.

Note: For a pleasant diversion from Rideau Canal exploration, visit the 325-hectare *Foley Mountain Conservation Area* ($ for parking), close to the village, and take a short walk to Spy Rock and its 180-degree panoramic view of the Rideau Lakes 60 metres below. Hiking on part of the Rideau

Trail and self-guided nature trails, a beach and group camping make this a popular outdoor spot.

Exploring the Rideau Canal from Westport to Kingston

The Rideau Canal strings lakes, rivers and artificial passages together like a string of sapphires between the head of Lake Ontario and the Ottawa River. Along the way, 49 locks carry pleasure vessels up or down as they travel along this serene waterway. Today's adventure includes must-stops at some of the most famous lock stations, so start out early to allow yourself two or three hours to browse around Kingston before the long journey back to Ottawa. Perhaps you'll want to stay over in the "Limestone City" for a night or two, as there's so much to see and do.

To begin a second day of Rideau Canal explorations, backtrack on Highway 42 from Westport to Crosby, and turn right onto Highway 15. Not far along, a sign indicating County Road 9 leads to *Chaffeys Locks*. Park near the late-1800s boathouse, and watch the boats being lifted or lowered three metres, not far from the former lockmaster's house, which now offers a glimpse into the past. Take a stroll through the grounds of the Opinicon Resort, the Chaffey family's early-nineteenth-century residence, and over the swing bridge to see the old mill. When returning to the highway, stop and wander through the cemetery to view the graves of canal builders who died of malaria.

Continue south and watch for the road at Elgin that goes to the *Davis Lock*, one of the most tranquil and idyllic spots on the Rideau Canal corridor. Follow the paved Davis Lock Road until it ends. Next, choose the gravel route that goes straight ahead and stay on it no matter what for eight kilometres, as it winds through some exquisite countryside to the place where many would like to spend a whole day watching canal traffic come and go.

A little further along the highway, don't miss the *Jones Falls Lock Station*. Park in the designated lot and take the stairs to the street below. Just past the Hotel Kenney, operated since 1877 by the same family, are the first three locks that take boats almost 18 metres up or down. Ascend the long flights of stairs to the interpretive display in the lockmaster's house, and then walk up the steep path to explore the Sweeney House and the blacksmith shop (cross the lock gate). Back on the other side of the canal, proceed up the road to see the 18.6-metre stone-arch dam on the way to the trail on the right that provides a short cut through fields of delicate wildflowers and hardwood forest, back to your vehicle.

If you wish, visit the Upper and Lower Brewer's Locks, located close to the highway, as you make your way to the last set of locks at *Kingston Mills*.

The locks at Jones Falls.

Plan to spend time watching luxurious yachts and canoes navigate the four locks, learning more about the construction of the canal at the historic blockhouse and interpretive centre.

From here, it's just a short drive south to Highway 2, and *Kingston*, the city of limestone. Back in 1857, Queen Victoria had a difficult decision to make: which city—Toronto, Kingston, Ottawa, Montreal or Quebec City—should be the capital of the Province of Canada? Of course you know the rest. Ottawa received the honour over this beautiful spot on the shores of Lake Ontario.

Drive past Fort Henry, which was built to prevent American attack and later used to protect the entrance to the canal. Before deciding if you want to visit the fort, continue over the causeway across the Cataraqui River into the downtown area.

Consider hopping on the Confederation Trolley ($), operated by the City of Kingston, to get a quick overview of this vibrant city. Later, if it's Tuesday, Thursday or Saturday, stop at the farmer's market nearby behind city hall to pick up some vegetables, fruit and baking to enjoy at one of the beautiful parks along Lake Ontario, the grounds of famous Queen's University, or wherever your travels take you the rest of the day.

Alternatively, stretch your legs by strolling around the city core, or taking King Street East and Front Road towards the airport to reach the Lemoine Point Conservation Area operated by the Cataraqui Region Conservation Authority. Here, forest, fields and spectacular water views provide a tranquil spot for a hike on 11 kilometres of trails.

Other options include renting a sailboat, canoe, kayak or sailboard close to the Pump House Steam Museum on Ontario Street to experience Lake Ontario for yourself, or boarding a cruise boat east of the park across from city hall to sail among the picturesque Thousand Islands.

When ready to head back to Ottawa, make your way to the north side of Kingston and travel west on Highway 401 to County Road 10 (Exit 617). Take the Old Perth Road, as it is sometimes known, through beautiful countryside and beside several lakes and on into Westport and *Perth*. Named after the city in Scotland, this charming town with its magnificent stone buildings is a great spot to get out of the car for awhile. Take a look around before setting out for downtown Ottawa via the quickest route—Highway 7 and Highway 417 East. Exit at Metcalfe Street.

Gatineau Park Treasures

Start: From downtown Hull, take Laurier Street and Alexandre-Taché Boulevard to the Gatineau Park entrance. Drive to the Welcome Area.
Route: Hilly, paved, two-lane roads.

> ### Hint
> All or part of this 45.5-kilometre park circuit makes for fabulous raise-your-heart-rate cycling, especially during Sunday Bikedays. At other times, leave your car at any of the hiking-trail parking lots to cycle an abbreviated version of the route, or take two vehicles and leave one at each end of your planned path.

Gatineau Park is a place for all seasons and all reasons. Annually, 1.5 million visitors come to cycle, hike, in-line skate, swim, camp, cross-country ski, snowshoe, picnic, or just contemplate nature.

Some residents living nearby visit this fabulous part of the park to show off the highlights to their out-of-town guests. Follow the route they might take to find hiking trails, sightseeing spots or swimming haunts. Depending on your mood, you choose where to stop.

From the park's *Welcome Area*, take the Gatineau Parkway straight ahead, past lush fields and maple and sumac forests, as it begins winding up through the Gatineau Hills. Before long you'll pass the *Hickory Trail*, a 20-minute jaunt on a wheelchair-accessible trail.

After a long climb, you reach the *Pink Lake Lookout*, a place to stop to see this gorgeous green lake, whose steep banks and 20-metre depth cause meromictic conditions. To have a closer look at this Gatineau Park highlight, continue on up the Parkway to the *Pink Lake Trail*, a pleasant 60-minute walking path around the lake.

Shortly beyond this spot, turn left onto the Champlain Parkway and continue alongside some very picturesque wetlands to reach a side entrance to the *Mackenzie King Estate*, the former home of Canada's longest-serving Prime Minister. King loved the Gatineau Hills so much that over the years he built Kingswood and Moorside. Go left to explore these properties, including the "architecture" King had installed, and to enjoy the beautiful English-style gardens and lunch in the tearoom ($ for parking in season).

Further along the parkway, watch for three hiking trails. From *Larriault Trail* or *Mulvihill Lake Trail* parking lots, it's about a one-hour's walk (add an hour if you want to visit the Mackenzie King Estate en route) along a scenic path beginning at one parking lot and ending at the other. *King Mountain Trail*, on the other hand, provides a pleasant 60-minute excursion along a more challenging interpretive trail that speaks about the forests that thrive in these parts.

Stop if you wish to have a peek at *Black Lake* and *Bourgeois Lake* before continuing on past the Fortune Lake Parkway turnoff. At the *Huron Lookout*, or my favourite, *Étienne-Brûlé Lookout*, enjoy a rest and perhaps a picnic in secluded and tranquil surroundings that offer a spectacular panorama of the Ottawa River Valley and the agricultural land of the Pontiac Region.

From here, you are close to the *Champlain Lookout*. Before taking the *Champlain Trail* down the Eardley Escarpment for a closer look, glance to the right to confirm that you're at the edge of the Gatineau Hills.

This is the turn-around point, so retrace your route to the Fortune Lake Parkway intersection. Turn left and go past the parking lot for the *Keogan Shelter*, one of the spots in the park where you can enjoy your meal indoors. For a change of scenery, pass some grassland on your way to Fortune Lake, and then it's down the steep and winding route to Dunlop Road.

Turn left here, and then left again onto Meech Lake Road. Consider a swim at *O'Brien Beach* ($ for parking). Alternatively, continue along the gravel road another four kilometres for a dip in the water at *Blanchet Beach*. When you're here, look high up on the cliffs to see Willson House, the famous site where Canada's constitutional negotiations took place in 1987.

Leave the beach area and journey back on Meech Lake Road. At the first intersection, turn left onto the Gatineau Parkway. At the stop sign, take the road through and past the *Penguin Picnic Grounds* and an ascent back to the Champlain Parkway intersection. Been there—done that, so veer left and stay on this parkway as you head back to the Welcome Area with a much better understanding of Gatineau Park, an integral part of Ottawa-Hull's fabric.

Note: When you're in the Gatineau Parkway/Meech Lake Road area, it's fun to visit the charming village of Old Chelsea. There you'll find the Gatineau Park Visitor Centre (call 819-827-2020), great restaurants, a bakery, art galleries, antique shops and a quick way to scoot back to Hull without finishing the driving loop if you want.

The Plaisance Area is Very Pleasant

Start: From Hull, take Highway 50 and Highway 148 past Masson and Thurso to Plaisance.
Route: Circle the area on main and secondary highways.

> **Hint**
> Don't forget your sports equipment.

This outing is all about choices—choices that you need to make and prepare for before setting out for Plaisance, a beautiful west-Quebec town in the Francophone Petite-Nation region. You could enjoy a delightful sightseeing trip to famous and beautiful spots in the area and then top the day off with an evening of French theatre. Or, what about doing a bit of sightseeing by car and then adding some cycling, swimming, mountain biking or horseback riding to make this a "participaction" kind of day.

Whatever you decide, bring what you need or make reservations before setting out for Plaisance, a settlement that started out as North Nation Mills in the early 1800s. Back then Joseph Papineau, seigneur of the area, decided to open a sawmill at *Plaisance Falls*, in the heart of the lush, green, mixed forest that blankets these parts. Years later, the Gatineau Power Company bought this property, so the village took roots where it stands today.

A delightful spot at which to begin your explorations is the old mill itself, located by turning north off Highway 148 at the flashing traffic light. Continue on Rue Papineau and Rang Malo to the falls ($), an ideal spot to hang out for awhile beside the thundering water. Enjoy a snack at one of the tables, or take the short walk down to the river's edge. Although there's a dock here, swimming is unsupervised and dangerous.

If you would prefer to look around the beautiful Petite-Nation River on horseback instead, call 819-427-9096 to arrange a trail ride or overnight camping expedition ($) that leaves from the bridge near the falls.

Back close to Highway 148 again, bird-watchers may enjoy investigating the *Plaisance Faunique Reserve* by car or bicycle, especially when hundreds of migrating Canada geese stop here each autumn. Two routes have potential for cyclists. For both, park at the village's information centre, and go south at the flashing light for a pleasant 2.5-kilometre journey along Chemin des Presqu'iles to the bike-path sign.

From here, the first cycling route takes you along a three-kilometre path that's perfect for spotting feathered creatures and taking a stroll on the boardwalk out over the marsh (there's a bike rack). At the end of the cycling path, go for a dip in the pool before heading back to your vehicle.

For a longer cycle, proceed as before, but don't take the bike path just yet. Instead, continue right along the road to find a gorgeous swamp, the Ottawa River and several bird-observation platforms. Turn left at the Montée Chartrand (beside the house with the cross), and follow the gravel road to the second camping area. Go for a swim in the pool or rent a canoe here before joining the bike path at its far end for the ride back towards the village.

To continue your Petite-Nation explorations from Plaisance, proceed 12 kilometres further east on Highway 148 to Montebello. Poke around *Manoir Papineau* ($), a national historic site, on the 26,305-hectare seventeenth-century seigneury located on the shores of the Ottawa River. Louis-Joseph Papineau, feudal lord of the Petite-Nation between 1846 and 1850 and son of the Plaisance sawmill owner, built this grand three-story manor.

Not far away, take a peek into the largest log cabin in the world, *Le Château Montebello*, to see the six-sided stone fireplace in the grand foyer. This historic year-round resort ($) also offers a variety of outdoor activities for both its guests and the general public. Fishermen should inquire about Kenauk. For information, call 819-423-6341, or 1-800-441-1414.

At the area's main tourist information centre, located in the old railway station on Highway 148, secure a map before challenging the steep and muddy, intermediate to expert mountain-bike trails. Take Rue St. Dominique, across from the information office, to reach the trail's start. For details, call 819-423-5602.

For those who enjoy observing wild animals in their natural habitat, take Highway 323 North to *Parc Oméga* ($). From the safety of your vehicle, you may be lucky enough to see moose, wapiti, bison, raccoons or even a black bear along the ten-kilometre road that winds through the 1,500-acre wilderness park. To reach the park, call 819-423-5487, or visit www.parc-omega.com.

Rather than retracing your route to Hull, circle back off the beaten track to discover fabulous agricultural sights with a touch of the Québécois influence, up against a stunning backdrop of deep-green rolling hills. Go north on Highway 323 and then left at the sign for *St-André-Avellin*, after crossing the Petite Rivière Rouge.

Continue along the village's main street and then left at the Halte Bernard Pilon picnic spot and on to *Ripon*. In the village, turn left four kilometres towards Montpellier to reach *La Ferme Lipial* (on Lussier Road), where dinner and French theatre or other entertainment ($) are featured certain warm-weather evenings in an old barn setting. Plan to make this a springtime sugar-shack stop. The phone number is 1-877-983-1717.

To return to Ottawa-Hull, drive back towards Ripon, and take Highway 317 to Thurso about 25 kilometres away. Turn right onto Highway 148 for the return journey to Hull. If you prefer a change of scene, drive as far as Masson and take the ferry across to Cumberland, on the Ontario side of the Ottawa River (operates 24 hours a day year round). Highway 174 West will then take you to Ottawa-Hull at the end of a long fun-filled day.

Exploring the Pontiac

Start: From downtown Hull, take Highway 148 West (drive left along Laurier Street, Alexandre-Taché Boulevard and Aylmer Road. Turn right at Park Street and then onto Eardley Road).
Route: The circuit travels on well-maintained Quebec highways.

Pontiac country, in western Quebec, is beautiful and steeped in history. As you journey west along Highway 148, notice the spectacular Eardley Escarpment that frames the southwest end of Gatineau Park. In the distance, catch a glimpse of the Ottawa River or Rivière des Outaouais, as it is known in French. Named after an Algonquin tribe, this major waterway carried lumber and fur in days gone by.

> **Hints**
> Bring your camera. Consider a sleepover at Cushing Nature Retreat's B and B, or a white-water rafting excursion.

Coulonge Falls

Continue west, past the road that leads to the spectacular Luskville Falls hiking trail in Gatineau Park and on into *Shawville*. It's worth stopping for a casual walk along Main and Centre Streets and Victoria Avenue to admire the heritage red-brick houses. At one time, two brick factories kept many area citizens employed; today this village is the commercial centre of the Pontiac, and each Labour Day weekend the site of one of the largest country fairs in Eastern Ontario or Western Quebec.

Further west on Highway 148, the route passes the region's administrative headquarters (including the tourist office, which you can reach at 1–800–665-5217) at *Campbell's Bay*, and several small villages in the agri-culturally rich, primarily bilingual Pontiac.

It's in this vicinity, near the Île du Grand Calumet and upstream on both sides of the Ottawa River, that people from all over the world come to challenge the frothing white water in rafts or kayaks. Unfortunately, there's not a good place to watch this thrilling adventure sport from the shore, but it's more fun to take part anyway. See the section on white-water rafting to sign up for some water-in-your-face excitement.

Proceed along the highway to find *Fort Coulonge*, an interesting town that was founded hundreds of years ago as a fur-trading post. Later, George Bryson, a lumber baron and prominent politician, arrived and left his mark. Walk Rue Principale to see the large stone mansions built for his family members. To see his own white, wooden, palatial home, continue along this road and through the *Marchand Bridge*. At 129 metres, this one-lane pine structure over the picturesque Coulonge River was originally built to link the region's lumbering areas to the town. Get out the camera for a photo of the second-longest covered bridge in the province.

Go right for a bit on Highway 148 to explore the Bryson home and then continue west again and take a short detour left on Thomas-Lefebvre Road to read more about the timber industry at the interpretive panels near the *Davidson Sawmill*. Back along 148, watch for the turnoff to the *Coulonge Falls* ($). Here, George Bryson built a 915-metre-long water chute to prevent the precious, squared-off white-pine logs from crashing over the falls that are almost 50 metres high. Today at the site, enjoy views from several lookout points, a walk through the woods or a picnic close to the thundering water. Call 819-683-2770.

This is the turn-around point, so head back to *Campbell's Bay*. Rather than returning to Hull the way you came, plan to take a traditional Sunday-afternoon-type drive through the beautiful and valuable forests that are the backbone of life in the Pontiac. Go left on Highway 301 past thousands of stately trees towards *Otter Lake*, watching for wildlife along the way. Before you get to the village, just past the lakes that front both sides of the high-way, turn right at the Union Cemetery onto Stephen Road. Turn right onto

Milliken Road and head up the mountain to visit the *Belle Terre Botanic Gardens*, and go for a nature walk if you want a break out of the car. You can reach the gardens at 819-453-7270.

Later, take a drive in to Otter Lake, and then travel south on Highway 303 towards *Ladysmith*, the site of Octoberfest on the weekend before Thanksgiving. You're now not far from the 250-hectare Cushing Nature Retreat. Call ahead to arrange a sleepover year round at this conservation spot that's the perfect venue for learning more about the natural world and the raptors that are bred and rehabilitated here on Indian Lake. You can call the retreat at 819-647-3226, or visit the website for more information at www.cushing-nature.com.

Once you're back in *Shawville*, proceed across Highway 148 toward the Ottawa River on Heath Road. Go left along Front Street and through *Bristol* and *Norway Bay* for a detour off the main drag through cottage country. Eventually, the route intersects Highway 148. Go right and trace your route back to Hull after a busy day away enjoying falls, forests and flowers.

Alternatively, to get back to Ottawa-Hull, travel into Quyon, a Pontiac village that celebrated its 125 anniversary in grand style in 2000. From here, take the ferry seven days a week across to Fitzroy Harbour on the Ontario side of the Ottawa River. From here it's about an hour on County Road 5 and Highway 417 into Ottawa.

Covered Bridges of the Gatineau Valley

Start: From Hull, travel north on Highway 5 to the Highway 105 North intersection.
Route: Consider Highway 105 the tree trunk. The bridges are hidden away on its gravel branches.

> **Hint**
> Bring a camera and a bathing suit.

Richard Kincaid found true love when he was photographing Madison County's covered bridges for *National Geographic*. Perhaps you will too, but it will be with the handsome wooden structures that were built between 1890 and 1930 to open up Quebec's interior.

When Richard left home, he took along his camera, a thermos and an ice chest. When setting out to visit them, pack these things as well and plan to stop along the way to pick up some great French-Canadian picnic fixings.

To find the first bridge, constructed with a roof and sides so that its frame would be protected from the harsh elements for up to a hundred years, watch for Pine Road on the left about half a kilometre past the traffic light at the Highway 105 North turnoff.

Go left here and then right onto Cross-Loop Road, for a trip beside lush forest and cow-dotted pastures that will take you down a steep incline to the attractive *Ruisseau Bridge* over Meech Creek. Built in 1924 and recently restored, it makes a picture-perfect logo to represent the magnificent surroundings of the 6,000 people who live in the Municipality of Chelsea.

Drive over the bridge and continue along this wandering country road until it intersects Highway 105 again. Turn left and proceed north to the sign for *Wakefield*, a charming village smack on the shore of the magnificent Gatineau River. Journey as far as the river and turn left to explore the galleries and restaurants that line its streets. Start gathering goodies at the Wakefield General Store to munch on later.

Since you're in town, go left off Riverside Drive on Mill Road to have a look at the old grist mill, which has been converted into the Wakefield Mill, a luxurious inn and conference centre. Cross the bridge beside it and go up the hill to *MacLaren's Cemetery* to see where Lester B. Pearson, Nobel Peace Prize winner in 1957 and prime minister of Canada from 1963–1968, is buried at the far end of row H, close to the woods.

Return to Riverside Drive again and go left. Soon you'll see the manual turntable where four men push the Hull-Chelsea-Wakefield Steam Train's 93-ton locomotive around for its 64-kilometre return journey to Hull each day, in season. Annually, about 50,000 passengers take this trip ($) that is especially popular for fall foliage and sunset dinner excursions. Information is available at 819-778-7246, or www.steamtrain.ca.

Proceed along the river through the village and turn right onto Highway 366 East. Immediately over the bridge, go right to find the 87-metre-long *Gendron Bridge*. The original structure built in 1915 was destroyed in a spectacular blaze set by an arsonist in 1984. Because the community greatly missed this historic landmark, by 1997 it was back in mint shape for use by pedestrians and bicycles, thanks to many hours of fund raising and volunteer work. Before leaving, go down the stairs to the left to shoot some photos of this beauty.

Later, retrace your route over the Highway 366 bridge. Turn right this time onto Highway 105 North and sit back and enjoy this scenic stretch alongside the Gatineau River. Just after the sign for Low, add some fudge to your picnic basket from the Pineview Restaurant.

Shortly thereafter, watch for the Magasin A. St. Jean (store) on your left. Turn left at the next road, called Fieldville, to begin a heavenly circuit at a leisurely pace through the back roads of the Gatineau Valley. Eventually, take a right onto Lyon Road and go right again on Pike Lake Road to find the magnificent *Kelly Bridge* punctuating the lush, green countryside with a splash of blood red. Get out your camera! Drive over the bridge and continue straight ahead on Pike Lake Road, a fair distance through this tranquil setting, all the way back to Highway 105.

Lester B. Pearson's Grave

Kelly Bridge

Go left once more, exploring the villages en route if you want. Just before Gracefield, turn left towards Cayamant after crossing the Picanoc Bridge, and then left again at Marks Road. Don't be fooled, thinking that the green bridge is your destination. Instead, continue to the Y intersection and take Cherry Creek Road right to the *Cousineau Bridge*, a pleasing structure with an interesting black-and-yellow frame defining its entrance. Take a walk to hear the gurgling stream before going back to Highway 105.

So far, every major directional sign since Hull says you're on the way to Maniwaki. Turn left and head 42 kilometres north to see what this place is all about. On the way, the highway passes through the *Kitigan Zibi Anisbinabeg Reserve*; stop to shop for unique beaded handicrafts and dream catchers.

Later, drive around *Maniwaki* to visit the Château Logue, a forest-preservation interpretive centre; the larger-than-life log-driver sculpture in Draveur Park; and the river-drive boat, Pythonga. One of the picnic tables along the Gatineau River may be the perfect spot to enjoy that fudge, if it made it this far.

At this point, you've been away from Hull about three-and-a-half hours and driven about 160 kilometres. As there are no bridges to visit on the way back, you'll cut 25 kilometres and about an hour and a half off the return journey. This said, if you turn back now you'll miss seeing two more attractive bridges and other special spots further up the road. The suggestions below, along with information from the Maniwaki Tourist Office, may help you decide. You might even consider an overnight stay here in the heart of logging country. Call 819-449-6627 for more information.

If you want to photograph more bridges, locate Manawaki's Dairy Queen, on the highway, and take Rue Principale Nord left through the residential area to the sign pointing the way to Zec Bras-Coupé Désert. Follow these signs ten kilometres to another of my favourites, the very-well-used *Montcerf Bridge*, vividly decked out in covered-bridge colours and later retrace your route back to Maniwaki.

At Grand Remous, 29 kilometres north of here on Highway 105, the sight of the *Savoyard Bridge* over the Gatineau River makes the drive worthwhile. Step back in time and pretend you're travelling by carriage through this picturesque structure soon after it was built in 1931. Go have a look at the rapids churning below the second-longest bridge seen today.

Not far from here, the *Baskatong Reservoir's* private beaches ($) offer a great cool-down spot if it's a hot day. This artificial lake's creation corresponds with the construction of the Mercier Dam.

If you take Highway 117 left instead, in less than an hour you'll be in the 13,610-square-kilometre *La Vérendrye Wildlife Reserve*, a wondrous wilderness that is home to 150 species of birds, black bears and a wide variety of fish and large game. The Mysterious Forest and the Roland Lake Falls a short distance into the park are star attractions. You can get detailed information at the park's entrance; call 1-800-665-6527 to reserve cabins and serviced camping.

A Day Away with a Difference

Start: From Ottawa, take Highway 417 and Highway 40 East to the first Rigaud exit. Proceed into the village, and follow the signs to the Shrine of Our Lady of Lourdes.
Route: Primarily uses four-lane highways.

Hint

Start out early, and bring sturdy walking shoes, a swimsuit and clothes suitable for fruit picking.

As you are driving to Montreal some night, look off in the distance shortly after passing the Ontario/Quebec border and you'll see a cross on top of Mount Rigaud, just east of the area where novice downhill skiers practice snowplows and parallel turns each winter. Taking a hike up the mountain to see this gigantic structure up close is a super way to begin a multi-tasking day.

If you stop to see the *Shrine of Our Lady of Lourdes*, an outdoor cathedral that resonates with music and prayer when people from around the world come to worship, you'll have permission to hike to the cross.

To get there, walk from the parking lot right, toward the forest. Look for interpretive panels at the start of the gravel trail and coloured crosses on rocks or tree trunks that mark the route as it ascends through the forest. A walking stick and your sturdy shoes will soon serve you well, as the path crosses veins of boulders here and there along the way. How unusual. Where did these come from?

Eventually the path intersects an old dirt road. Go left and under the power lines before picking up the trail on the right again. Follow this to a clearing and locate the steep flight of rock stairs up to the mountain's summit. Climb these cautiously to find a breathtaking, unobstructed view of the countryside spread before you. What a fabulous spot for a picnic!

Walk around the crown of the mountain and begin your descent via the path to the right as you face the valley. Proceed through the forest and stop to enjoy more panoramic scenes before turning right under the power lines and finding the path to retrace your steps.

When you reach the foot of the mountain, go up the paved path to the *Champs des Guérets* or devil's garden. Some say these rocks came to be here because a farmer plowed his potato field on the Sabbath and this offended God so much that he turned the peasant's crop into a blanket of stones. A more plausible explanation may be that this unique area was created eons ago when saltwater from the Champlain Sea pounded the glaciers.

After marvelling at the spread of boulders, take the path to view the tiny wooden chapel with the domed roof, before descending the stairs down to the main sanctuary again. Stop awhile to contemplate the wonders of nature at this open-air spot, which draws 125,000 pilgrims each year for services, celebrations, and the sound-and-light show, in French. I hope you get a chance to experience the out-of-this-world acoustics in this spectacular setting. Call 450-451-4631 for more information.

Later, leave the sanctuary grounds and go right on St-Jean-Baptiste, through the village of Rigaud. Continue straight (past the exit for Ottawa) about 20 minutes to *Hudson*. On the way, when you reach a Y intersection, take the left fork for a pleasant drive past magnificent homes and gardens. Stop at the historic Willow Place Inn on the shore of the Lake of Two Mountains for a bite, if you wish, before proceeding a short way further down the road to the *Oka Ferry* terminal. Drive on board ($) in anticipation of an hour or two picking McIntosh, Spartan, Delicious or Empire apples or other orchard fruits, in season, not far from the village. Call the tourist office for ideas before you leave home, at 450-479-8389.

Later, take the village's Notre-Dame and Oka Road west to the *Cistercian Abbey*, where a small group of fathers and brothers have lived since 1881. Take a walk around the peaceful gardens and shop for some of the monk's famous cheese.

If you feel like it, stop at *Oka Park* on the way back to the ferry to laze on the wonderful sandy beach. Keep your eye on the ferry schedule, though, so you're sure to be on board in time to get back to Hudson for the two-and-one-half-hour journey back to Ottawa before it gets dark (take Bellevue Boulevard and Daoust Road to reach Highway 40), after this unique day away in Western Quebec.

OUTDOOR
SPECTACLES

astern Ontario and Western Quebec have more outdoor festivals,
celebrations and other things going on than I ever remember taking
place within two hours of where I lived in Alberta. For example, each
weekend between June and mid October, there are often so many special
events scheduled that it's a toss up which to choose.

This section describes some of the best, starting with sugaring off, the rite
of spring in this part of Canada. Under this heading, details are provided
about several spots that host a sugarbush experience once the sap has started
to run. All other parts of this section follow a similar format.

As usual, directions to the various sites are often provided.
Approximate dates are indicated, but phone ahead or
check the website listed for precise dates, times and
admission fees before confirming your plans. Once you
figure in the time needed to get to there, many of these
outings will make full-day adventures.

Sugaring Off

In 1998, when an ice storm extraordinaire raged through Eastern Ontario and
Western Quebec, maple-syrup producers watched in horror. Branches of
their magnificent trees bowed to the forest floor under the terrific weight of
the ice, while limbs of others simply snapped like matchsticks. Many younger
trees gently arched over and never righted themselves again. Worst of all,
the crowns of the mighty maples suffered significant damage.

Despite this, collecting sap from maple trees with fewer taps continues in
March or April when the days are warm (two to eight degrees Celsius) and
the nights cold (minus two to minus seven degrees Celsius).

Sliding during Winterlude.

Begin a day in the sugarbush by finding a tree with sap dripping into an aluminum pail. Taste it before it becomes liquid gold, and then head off for a hike or horse–drawn sleigh ride ($) through the forest. End a truly Canadian outing with a feast of pancakes and sausages smothered in maple syrup.

One good place to experience sugaring off is in Lanark County—the maple syrup capital of Ontario. To reach *Wheelers Maple Products, Pancake House and Sugar Camp*, where about 9,000 trees are tapped annually, from Ottawa take Highway 417 and Highway 7 West past Carleton Place. Go right on County Road 15 and County Road 12 to the village of Lanark. Continue west toward McDonalds Corner and follow the signs. You can reach Wheelers at 278-2788, or visit www.wheelersmaple.com.

Fulton's Pancake House & Sugar Bush is a 400-acre sugar bush that is over 150 years old. Locate it by going west from Ottawa on Highway 417 and Highway 17 to Antrim. Go left on County Road 20 as far as the beautiful five-span stone bridge in Pakenham, and turn left onto County Road 29. Continue through the village and the countryside to Cedar Hill Side Road. Turn right and then left onto 6th Concession Road. Call 256-3867, or go to www.fultons.on.ca.

Elsewhere, visit the *Sucrerie de la Montagne*, about an hour and a quarter east of Ottawa, to enjoy sugaring off and traditional Québécois folk entertainment. To reach this heritage site, from Ottawa travel east on Highway 417 and Highway 40 and take Saint-Jean Baptiste toward Rigaud. Go right on Highway 325, left on Chemin de la Montagne and then left again on Rang St-Georges to number 300. For more information call 450-451-0831, or look up www.sucreriedelamontagne.com.

On the Quebec side of the Ottawa River, make *Cabane à Sucre Beauregard* a springtime destination to enjoy a truly Canadian experience once the sap is running. From Hull, take Highway 50 East to the Monteé Paiement Exit. Turn left and continue about ten kilometres. The phone number is 819-671-2354.

Flowers, Flowers, Flowers

When heliopsis, hollyhocks, hostas and hydrangea cohabit in Canadian gardens, soft and dramatic shades and shapes combine to make us thankful that some of us are born with a green thumb.

The Ottawa-Hull landscape hosts the first major visual feast of the season at *Canadian Tulip Festival* time, when parks, streets and yards come alive, as red tulips with yellow-edged, pointed petals burst into bloom alongside blossoms of deep purple, pure white and frosty pink.

This ten-day, mid-May event took root in 1945, when Princess Juliana of the Netherlands presented Canada with 100,000 tulip bulbs as thanks for liberating Holland from Nazi occupation during the Second World War, and

Collecting sap from a maple.

for the safe haven provided her family. Today, a million showy bulbs bloom annually during the largest flower festival in the world.

Hop the shuttle bus to see a rainbow-like display of 300,000 tulips at Commissioners Park at Dows Lake, 15,000 at the Canadian Museum of Civilization and 40,000 more at the Casino de Hull, amidst its illuminated fountains. Visit Parliament Hill, where hundreds of cardinal red tulips carpet the garden beneath the Peace Tower, to photograph a scene often associated with Canada's capital.

Nearby, Major's Hill Park showcases five hectares of blossoms, floral displays, family activities and musical events ($). On the Tulip Festival's last weekend, don't miss the Flotilla on the Rideau Canal between Dows Lake and the National Arts Centre. Call 567-4447 for information, or visit www.tulipfestival.ca.

Sometimes it's fun to enjoy beautifully created gardens, resplendent with orange azaleas, pink peonies, flowering crab apple trees and a profusion of sunny daffodils alongside art forms such as watercolour paintings, hand-woven linens and interesting sculptures. During the *Up the Garden Path Garden and Studio Tour*, held on both the Victoria and the United States Memorial Day weekends in May, flower and art lovers can do just that at various locales close to the picturesque Thousand Islands Parkway on the St. Lawrence River. For more information call 923-5452.

Towards the end of May, the lilac capital of Ontario comes alive with the sight and scent of 33 acres of wild lilacs. To celebrate these purple beauties, the *Franktown Lilac Festival* ($) features great country entertainment, food and fun. From Ottawa, travel west on Highway 417 and Highway 7 towards Carleton Place. Go left on Highway 15 to Franktown. Phone 283-4895, or visit sites.netscape.net/franktownlilacs/homepage.

Anyone with an interest in gardening should attend the special events held at *Gardens North* on the third weekend of each month, May through August. At the same time, wander the paths of the magnificent display gardens on the eight-acre site, whose seed harvest is later sold around the world. From Ottawa, travel west on Highway 417, and south on Highway 416 to Exit 57 (Manotick). Go right at the Brophy Road Exit and left on Third Line Road. Call 489-0065.

Up in the Laurentian Mountains, *Les Jardins de Mireille* ($) provides a tranquil and serene setting for visitors to commune with nature's beauty among the lilies, purple coneflowers, impatiens and tangles of clematis. From Hull, take Highway 50 and Highway 148 East to Montebello. Go north on Highway 323 to St-Jovite and then five kilometres south on Highway 327. Open June to October. Phone 819-425-2544.

The *Enchanted Gardens* ($), about an hour and a half west of Ottawa, offer a must-stop spot for flower lovers. As well, during their special workshop and lecture series, study up on healing herbs, arranging fresh-cut garden flowers, and using watercolours to bring nature's gifts into your living room. At any time, nature trails invite learning about the hardwoods blanketing the area, and theme gardens awaken the senses to perfect beauty. Before sitting down for a scrumptious meal at the 1800s London House, take a one-and-one-half-kilometre stroll to enjoy vistas of the mighty Ottawa River. From Ottawa, travel west on Highway 417 and Highway 17 to the Storyland Road Exit (County Road 4). Turn right and proceed to the Four Corners stop sign. Continue straight about ten kilometres, turn right at the garden's sign, and then on to the stop sign. Drive straight ahead over County Road 43 and the railway tracks to the gardens/River Run location. You can call the Enchanted Gardens at 646-2994 or 1-888-537-4259, or visit their website at www.enchantedgardens.on.ca.

Towards the end of June, a must-see floral event occurs when 16,000 showy lady's slipper orchids burst forth into a vibrant display of delicate pink and white blooms at the *Purdon Conservation Area*. This exceptional wetland also provides interpreters so you can get the most from your visit. From Ottawa, travel west on Highway 417 and Highway 7 to Perth. Take Highway 511 to Lanark, and go through the village to County Road 8. Turn left, travel about 14 kilometres to Concession Road 8 and go right about 3 kilometres. The second of the two parking lots offers wheelchair accessibility. For a blooming update call 259-2421.

Ottawans and visitors know that summer is here when they get a chance to take a peek at Rideau Hall's ornamental gardens, usually the last weekend of June. The annual *Governor General's Garden Party* features visits to the greenhouses that supply flowers for Canada's official residences, tours of Rideau Hall's public rooms and an opportunity to greet the governor general in the terraced gardens. While there, plan to photograph a few of the 300 varieties of fragrant roses in the Canadian Heritage Garden, and study the commemorative plaques posted under the oak and maple trees indicating the name of the visiting head of state, member of the royal family or other dignitary who planted that particular one. From downtown Ottawa, take Sussex Drive to Rideau Gate and park on the nearby streets. Call 991-4422 or 1-866-842-4422, or visit www.gg.ca.

The *Mackenzie King Estate Garden Party* ($) gives guests a chance to relive the '20s, '30s and '40s on its magnificently manicured grounds. Held in mid August, highlights include a vintage fashion show, antique cars, and tours of Canada's tenth prime minister's country estate. From Hull, take Highway 5 North to Exit 12. Turn left and proceed through Old Chelsea. Go left onto the Gatineau Parkway and follow the signs. For more information call 819-827-2020 or 1-800-465-1867, or go to www.capcan.ca.

Art in Gatineau Park, held on two mid-August weekends, features an art exhibition and sale in a summery garden resplendent with pastel gladiolas and purple coneflowers. From Hull, take Highway 5 North exiting at Hautes Plaines. Continue west to its end and turn right, proceeding 2.5 kilometres on what becomes Mine Road. Turn right on Solitude Road North and look for number 79. Call 819-827-3489 for details.

Pomp and Ceremony

In today's world, certain things are just not like they used to be. On the other hand, thank goodness some things never seem to change. For example, the military parade still boasts colour, precision, pageantry and music—enough signature ingredients to send shivers down your spine, as men and women in smartly pressed uniforms move left, right, left in perfect time. Each summer in historic Eastern Ontario, opportunities to photograph these magnificent spectacles abound.

The *Changing of the Guard on Parliament Hill* showcases Canadian tradition at its colourful best from late June to late August. Starting at 9:30 A.M., members of the Governor General's Foot Guards and the Canadian Grenadier Guards march up Elgin Street to the Hill in their scarlet tunics and tall bearskin hats in time for the 10:00 A.M. ceremony. Come early to secure a good spot to enjoy the military music and proceedings. For details, call 239-5000 or 1-800-465-1867, or go to www.capcan.ca.

Marching to Parliment Hill.

These regiments also stand guard at Rideau Hall, the governor general's residence. See the *Relief of the Sentry* ceremony, staged hourly at both the main gate and in front of the mansion. As well, as a climax to the changing-of-the-guard season, attend the *Trooping of the Colour* to see the inspection of the guard and the march past. From downtown Ottawa, take Sussex Drive to Rideau Gate. Call 991-4422 or 1-866-842-4422, or visit the website at www.gg.ca.

Be ready for the sound of the cannon on three mid-July evenings when Parliament Hill comes alive with the sound of pipe bands, military music and gunners during the *Canadian Forces Massed Band Retreat*. For more information call 239-5000 or 1-800-465-1867, or see www.capcan.ca.

Another Ottawa, warm-weather highlight for residents and visitors alike is the Sunset Ceremony of the world-famous *Royal Canadian Mounted Police Musical Ride*. The evening's performance, presented once each summer, also includes dressage, show jumping and lively band music. From downtown Ottawa, take Sussex Drive and the Rockcliffe Parkway to Birch Avenue and turn right to the RCMP stable grounds. Bring the family and a blanket or lawn chairs. For more information call 993-3751, or go to www.rcmp-grc.gc.ca.

Further away from the capital, military music, precision drills, artillery exercises and a colourful fireworks finale make the *Fort Henry Sunset Ceremonies* ($) the place to be in Kingston each Wednesday evening during July and August. The fort, constructed by the British in the early 1800s to guard against American attack, stands proudly on a hill overlooking the city and Lake Ontario. From Ottawa, take Highway 417 West, and Highway 416 South to Kemptville. Go west on Highway 43 and south again on Highway 15 from Smiths Falls. Go right on Highway 2 and then left at the traffic light to the fort. (On the right watch for Canada's Royal Military College, on the opposite bank of Navy Bay as you go up the hill). You can reach the fort at 542-7388, or visit the website at www.forthenry.com.

Mostly Music

Eastern Ontario and Western Quebec showcase long, hot, lazy summers—summers perfect for hanging out on a lawn chair with your bare feet caressing the cool, damp grass and the moon and the stars as your companions while the music plays on. Here's the scoop on some great outdoor gigs where you can overdose on tunes.

For all engagements charging admission, the routine is the same. Buy a value-priced, all-event pass up front at the designated ticket outlet, exchange this for a bracelet at the gate, come early to secure a top piece of real estate, and stay late until the last song is but a memory. If there's space, you may also procure a day ticket at the gate. Don't forget something to sit on, and

Bluesfest

some sunscreen and a hat; if you plan to be there after the sun goes down, tuck a sweater into your pack. As well, bring along a picnic (no glass allowed) or plan to chow down on samosas, fajitas, gourmet ice cream or finger-licking fresh-fruit chocolate fondue if there's a food fair at the event.

Beginning around Canada Day, about half-a-dozen free afternoon or early evening concerts performed throughout the summer draw thousands of music aficionados to the expansive lawn of *Rideau Hall*, the Ottawa home of Canada's governor-general, on Rideau Gate just off Sussex Drive. Pack an early dinner or snack to enjoy outdoors. For more information call 991-4422 or 1-866-842-4422, or visit www.gg.ca.

In early July, the *Ottawa Bluesfest* ($) kicks off the major music-festival scene in Eastern Ontario and Western Quebec. Close to a hundred-thousand blues lovers hunker down to hear the best of the blues and gospel during the second-largest event of its kind in North America (the biggest is in Chicago). This finger-snapping party takes place at LeBreton Flats, not far from the city's downtown core. Call 247-1188, or check out www.ottawa-bluesfest.ca.

Later in July, the Laurentian Mountains come alive with the sound of the blues when the three-day *Tremblant International Blues Festival* ($) comes to the village and base of the ski hill. From Hull, take Highway 50 and Highway 148 East to Montebello. Go north on Highway 323 to St-Jovite and then left on Highway 117 North past the village about two kilometres to Montée Ryan. Turn right and follow the signs. For more information call 819-681-2000 or 1-888-736-2526, or visit www.tremblant.ca.

For those who prefer a softer, more improvisational sound, the *Ottawa International Jazz Festival* ($) is guaranteed to provide pleasant memories. Big-name and local jazz artists fill the ten-day bill at downtown Confederation Park and other venues around the city beginning in mid July. For details call 241-2633 or visit www.jazz.ottawa.com.

Later in the month, an eclectic variety of performing artists entertain thousands on the banks of the picturesque Tay River during Perth's three-day *Stewart Park Festival* ($). From Ottawa, take Highway 417 and Highway 7 West to Perth. Call 264-1190 or go to www.mapleweb.com/stewartparkfest.

In late August, various spots throughout Kingston are jumping when the *Limestone Blues Festival* ($) livens up the music scene. From Ottawa, take Highway 417 West, and Highway 416 South to Kemptville. Go west on Highway 43 and south on Highway 15 from Smiths Falls. Call 548-4415 or 1-888-855-4555, or visit www.kingstoncanada.com.

At about the same time, over 200 musicians take to the stage to sing about real life and its challenges at *Ottawa's Folk Festival* ($) in Britannia Park, on the shore of the Ottawa River. From downtown, go west on the Ottawa River Parkway and Carling Avenue to Greenview Avenue. Turn right. More information is available at 230-8234, or at www.ottawafolk.org.

To top off the busy summer music season, plan to attend the free outdoor concerts at *La Fête de la Musique* on Labour Day weekend. Tap your toes to tunes by an eclectic slate of musicians from around the world who play at Mont Tremblant in the Laurentians. To get there and for contact details, check the directions for the Blues Festival above.

Much More Than Music

People in this part of Canada love music so much that on select summer weekends they attend outdoor musical happenings in droves. By now, you should know the drill—buy a pass for the whole affair or line up at the gate for a one-shot ticket. At many of these extravaganzas, there's a bonus— activities unique to an area share top billing alongside great bands and tasty festival eats. Load the lawn chairs and the family, and come early to settle in for some toe-tapping, hand-clapping, hip-swinging fun. When you're packing, if the event's near the water, consider bringing a light jacket if you're planning to stay late.

Brockville, on the scenic shore of the St. Lawrence River, is stage central for *Riverfest* ($) for five days on and around July 1. Besides nightly concerts and stage shows, plan on attending the high-diving hydroplane races and outdoor theatre. From Ottawa, take Highway 417 West, Highway 416 South and Highway 2 West. Call 342-8975, or visit www.recorder.ca/riverfest.

Forty-thousand people have already discovered that the four-day *Buckingham en Fête* ($) is the place to be in mid July. Join them to enjoy French and English musical performances and activities for the whole family. From Hull, travel east on Highway 50 and then north on Highway 309 to Buckingham, about 25 minutes away. For information call 819-986-4204.

On the other side of the Ottawa River and east a bit, the five-day *Wendover Western Festival* ($) has attracted people from far and wide for more than 15 years. Get the RV gang together the third weekend in July to see western artists, fiddlers, and step dancers entertain. From Ottawa, take Highway 417 and Highway 174 East to Wendover. Call 673-5070.

Why not complete your summertime musical schedule with a concert on the waterfront of the St. Lawrence River. Be there each August during the ten-day *Festival of the Islands* ($) to enjoy nightly performances by top entertainers and the Gananoque Skydivers. At other times during the event, take in the parade, model-railroad show, midway, historical re-enactments, mini-poker run on the river, and the last evening's gigantic fireworks display. From Ottawa, take Highway 417 West, and Highway 416 South to Kemptville. Go west on Highway 43, south again on Highway 15, and then Highway 32. Call 382-1562 for details or visit www.gananoque.com/festival.

Celebrating Our Heritages

Residents of Eastern Ontario and Western Quebec, whose family roots span the globe, make the area's cultural tapestry rich and diverse. Each year, celebrations honouring these ties give the rest of us a chance to learn more about the heritage, traditions and specialty cuisine that make our neighbours and friends the special people they are.

It was the native Canadians who were the first to ply the Ottawa River in their birch-bark canoes. For over 25 years now, people of various First Nations have come together to celebrate this proud aboriginal heritage at the *Odawa Pow Wow* ($). The Grand Entry Procession and dance competitions, with the dancers in their finest regalia, are must-sees at this very popular event held on the May weekend following Victoria Day. Bring your camera and don't be too shy to participate in the social dances when invited. From Ottawa, take Highway 417 West to Moodie Drive and go north and then left to reach the Ottawa-Nepean Tent and Trailer Park, 411 Corkstown Road. Call 722-3811 or visit www.odawa.on.ca.

West of Ottawa, don't let another summer end without attending and participating in the *Pikwakanagan First Nation's Pow Wow* ($), the third weekend in August. Again, many nations will be uniting and dancing in their colourful regalia, to the call of the drum, at a spiritual site nestled among the birch and cedars. Native cuisine and the sale of unique aboriginal handicrafts add to the atmosphere at this traditional event. From Ottawa, take Highway 417 West and Highway 17 to the Highway 60 junction. Turn left and follow it to Golden Lake. For details call 625-2519 or 1-800-897-0235, or go to www.atapik.com.

In mid June, all of us who wish we were Italian can join in the *Italian Week* celebrations with those who claim that heritage. Make the Preston Street neighbourhood party-time headquarters to watch a game of bocce or soccer, listen to some Italian music, take in a colourful dance performance or enjoy a pasta dinner. Call 235-2908.

For both Anglophones and Francophones, a *Saint Jean Baptiste Day* celebration provides the perfect place for the whole family to enjoy Québécois entertainment for three days annually around June 24. Both Hull's Mousette Park and Aylmer's Park des Cadres also feature parades and other outdoor activities. Call 819-778-2222.

If you can't make it to either of these Quebec parties, try to catch up with the French-speaking musicians and visual and performing artists that are entertaining during the *Franco-Ontarien Festival* in Ottawa for several days in and around the same time period. Phone 741-1225, or visit www.ffo.ca.

For a wee taste of Scotland, gather the whole clan and head for the *Glengarry Highland Games* ($) the weekend before the first Monday in

Pow Wow

August. Friday evening's spectacular tattoo features pomp and ceremony, massed bands and Scottish dancers. Saturday, the beauty and tradition of the highland dance and pipe-band championships share the field with kilt-clad, strong men from across the continent that are putting stones and sheaves, throwing 7.2-kilogram hammers and tossing the caber. Take Highway 417 East, and Highland Road (Exit 51) south to Maxville. For more information call 527-2876, or visit www.glengarryhighlandgames.com.

In late August, a smaller but nonetheless spectacular Scottish event happens in Almonte during the *North Lanark Highland Games* ($). Bagpipes, highland dance competitions, heavyweight events and a ceilidh (Scottish party) make this a special occasion near the banks of the scenic Mississippi River. From Ottawa, take Highway 417 West, and Highway 49 South (March Road). Call 256-2064, or go to www.almontehighlandgames.inawire.com.

In mid August, get into the mood to visit the sunny Mediterranean by attending the ten-day *Greek Cultural Summer Festival*. Be on hand for Zorba's dish-breaking dance, traditional Greek dancing and a tasty helping of souvlaki, skewered lamb or baklava. Call 225-8016, or visit www.helleniccommunity.com.

To round off a season of cultural festivals, don't spend your hard-earned cash on a trip to Germany. Instead, make tracks for Avonmore to attend the first *Oktoberfest* in the Ottawa–Hull area on Saturday of the second weekend in September ($). Enjoy tasty homemade German food before the dancing begins. From Ottawa, travel on Highway 417 East, Highway 138 and Highway 43 West. Call 436-2252 for information.

Then, if you're on hand the first weekend in October at Ladysmith in Quebec's Pontiac Region ($), you can enjoy more oomp-pa-pa music, tasty sausages, sauerkraut, Black Forest cake, and the many outdoor activities that have delighted thousands for 15 years. From downtown Hull, take Highway 148 West (drive left along Laurier Street, Alexandre-Taché Boulevard and Aylmer Road. Turn right at Park Street and then onto Eardley Road) and proceed on to Shawville. Go north on Highway 303. For information call 819-647-5306.

Buskers, Balloons and Bursts of Colour

Each year when I'm planning my summer festival-going schedule, I try to add some events other than music to my calendar. Eastern Ontario and Western Quebec have no shortage of unique outdoor spectacles to fill this bill. All are festivals with excitement, festivals that entertain, and festivals that have made thousands come back time and time again. Many are family affairs so the whole gang can come along. For some you need a ticket up front, but for others you just show up when you're in the mood for some fun.

Every summer night there's a festival of sorts happening on sedate Parliament Hill, when the area comes to life after dark during the *Sound and Light Show*.

Busker's Festival

Be in the bleachers when the Parliament Buildings become the stage as Canada's story is told to Canadians and guests from around the globe. Find out more by calling 239-5000 or 1-800-465-1867, or by checking out www.capcan.ca.

On July 1 each year, the Hill is also the centre attraction. Don your red and white and head that way to take part in a jam-packed day of entertainment and special displays during the biggest birthday party held in the entire country. If you want to be up front for the fabulous fireworks display that provides the climax to the *Canada Day* celebrations, set out for Major's Hill Park well before 10:00 P.M. to secure a great view of Nepean Point.

On Sparks Street, not far from Parliament Hill, colourful clowns, talented jugglers, brazen fire eaters and sleight-of-hand magicians wow admiring crowds gathered for the *Ottawa International Busker Festival* each August Civic Holiday weekend. Bring along a pocketful of toonies to show your appreciation. For information call 230-0984.

At the *Buskers Rendezvous* in Kingston, expect the unexpected for three days each July. Friday and Saturday shenanigans will provide plenty of laughs; Sunday's grande finale is a must-see performance. From Ottawa, take Highway 417 West and then Highway 416 South to Kemptville. Go west on Highway 43 and south again on Highway 15 from Smiths Falls. Call 548-4415 or 1-888-855-4555, or go to www.kingstonarea.on.ca.

On another festival front, for five select mid-summer evenings the fire moves from street level to the sky, as the heavens over Leamy Lake brilliantly sparkle with showers of red, white, blue and green during the *Casino de Hull Sound of Light* ($). Buy a reserved seat or a beach spot to be among those marvelling at this international fireworks competition that comes complete with musical synchronization. Parking is limited, so take the shuttle. Or, from Hull, drive north on Highway 5, exit at St-Joseph South and follow the signs. For information phone 819-771-3389.

There are always fireworks of a different sort when *Odyssey Theatre Under the Stars* ($) takes to the Strathcona Park stage for a one-month, mid-summer run. For over 15 seasons, some of the best Commedia dell' Arte (Italian mask theatre) there is keeps performing art's lovers returning year after year. Plan to be on the banks of the Rideau River (Laurier Avenue East and Range Road) for a warm summer evening's worth of laughter and tears. Call 232-8407.

To wrap up the all-too-short summer in top style, the place to be on the Labour Day weekend is the *Gatineau Hot Air Balloon Festival* ($). The four-day event showcases about 150 gigantic dinosaurs, apples, shopping carts, cows and multi-coloured balloons sailing up, up and away into the early morning or late afternoon sky. For those with their feet still on the ground, nightly concerts, magicians, midway rides and clowns entertain. From Hull, take Highway 148 East. Go north on Gréber Boulevard and east on Saint Louis to La Baie Park. For details call 819-243-2330 or 1-800-668-8383, or visit www.ville.gatineau.qc.ca.

Food Festivals

When it comes to gastronomic festivals, I consider the *Festival of the Maples* to be the party to kick off the season in these parts. Everyone, young and old, is invited to the grand finale of yet another successful Lanark County sugaring-off season. No need to R.S.V.P.—just be in historic Perth the last Saturday in April to celebrate the arrival of spring once the last sap has dripped from the stately maples. The syrup producers will be on hand for sure, competing for top honours in several classes. Add the final touch to a perfect day by pouring some thick, golden "made in Canada" maple syrup on a stack of fluffy pancakes at the breakfast, and then take in the fiddling, step dancing and children's rides. From Ottawa, take Highway 417 and Highway 7 West to Perth. Call 267-3200.

A couple of months later, find out why gourmet cooking has replaced lots of humdrum meat-and-potato feasts in Canadian homes. Many a home chef is copying what the professionals knew all along—use fresh herbs and you'll add zest, flavour and oomph to many a culinary delight. Each July during *Herbfest* ($), stroll the Herb Garden's displays, accompanied by the distinct aroma of sage, rosemary, thyme, oregano and basil, to learn some of the secrets. From Ottawa, take Highway 417 and Highway 7 West, and turn right on Upper Dwyer Hill Road. Continue six kilometres and then go right to reach 3840 Old Almonte Road. The Herb Garden can be reached at 256-0228, or at www.herbgarden.on.ca.

A few weeks later, if you love garlic and want to learn more about growing and using this pungent bulb in that special dish at your next dinner party, be at this event to find out why "it's chic to reek." At the *Perth Garlic Festival* ($) each August, sample some garlic-laced foods, take in the cooking demonstrations and add some entertainment to round off a fun Saturday or Sunday outing. From Ottawa, take Highway 417 and Highway 7 West to Perth. For details call 267-5322 or 1-877-268-2833, or go to www.perthgarlicfestival.com.

In Carp, much closer to Ottawa-Hull, follow your nose to another party where garlic's the most important guest of the day. The *Garlic Festival of Eastern Ontario* ($) is sure to be serving up food seasoned with this delicious and healthy relative of the onion on a fine August weekend. Entertainment of all sorts will make you glad you came from Ottawa, along Highway 417 West to the Carp Exit (number 155). For information, call 264-0364 or visit www.garlicfestival.on.ca

Never turn down an invitation to a party, especially not when there's a chance to find out more about cheese from those in the know since 1894. At the *St. Albert's Curd Festival* ($), held annually in mid August, spend a day in the country sampling some of their famous cheddar, listening to a few tunes and trying your luck at bingo during the four-day celebration. From Ottawa, take Highway 417 East to Exit 79. Go south to St. Albert. For information, call 987-2872 or 1-800-465-1553.

Country Fairs

The warm-weather season just isn't complete without at least one day at a country fair. These grand community social gatherings took root back in the 1800s, when farmers gathered to show off their cows and horses in hopes of proving theirs the best. At the same time, Mom and the kids decided to exhibit their talents as well.

Although the country fair has evolved since then, its basic agricultural and handicraft core remains the same. Years ago, my grade 6 handwriting hung proudly in the Calgary Exhibition and Stampede's exhibition hall, not far from the pink-and-blue crocheted layettes, gorgeous cross-stitched cushions, daintily embroidered pillow slips and shining jars of mustard relish. These days, displays of "my best printing", intricately iced cakes, homemade wines and attractive flower arrangements sport the coveted red, blue and white ribbons alongside the biggest pumpkins and best tomatoes in the neighbourhood.

Arrive early in the day to take a tour of these labours of love, and then choose a spot ringside to watch the area's farmers parade their finest sheep, cows and heavy horses. Include at least one of the 4-H (Heart, Hands, Health and Head) livestock competitions, to share the pride of these young Canadians.

Livestock competition at a country fair.

Later, perhaps you'll see a horse or antique-tractor pull, a parade, the Raisin River foot race or even a beard-growing contest. Later, to round out a perfect fair-going day, it's off to the midway for a game or five of bingo and a round on the ferris wheel.

Head for Williamstown to attend a fair that's been held since 1812, or take in events at one of its younger counterparts that are still well over 150 years old. Here's a list of some of the more popular ones within a two-hour drive of Ottawa-Hull. Each occurs at about the same time every year, so these 2000 dates give you an idea of when that is. Call ahead for exact details ($) or check the daily or weekly newspapers for up-to-date particulars.

June	Maxville	527-5346
June 7–11	Gloucester	741-3247
July 21–23	Avonmore	346-2252
July 28–30	Beachburg	646-7198
July 28–31	Delta	928-2800
August	Winchester	989-1575
August 10–13	Navan	835-2766
August 11–13	Arnprior	623-9663
	Williamstown	931-3110
August 25–27	Chesterville	448-3546
Labour Day weekend	Perth	267-4104

Labour Day weekend	Shawville	819-647-3213
September 6–10	Renfrew	432-5331
September 7–10	Russell	445-3079
September 8–10	Almonte	256-2034
September 14–17	Kingston	542-6701
September 15–17	Richmond	838-3420
September 21–24	Carp	839-2172
September 28–October 1	Metcalfe	821-0591

For those who prefer a taste of the country on a much larger scale, Ottawa's ten-day Central Canada Exhibition ($) offers it all—cotton candy, corn dogs, kid's world, agricultural exhibits, 4-H competitions, youth talent, top-name entertainment, games of chance, roller coasters and rides that'll make you flip. Dates for 2000 were August 17 to 27. To find out more, call 237-7222.

Wintertime Fun

When the snow's flying and the weather cold and crisp, conditions are ideal for frolicking in the outdoors. At first it may seem a bit too chilly to venture far from the fireplace and television, but once you get going I guarantee that an invigorating day in the fresh air will make you glad you moved from the couch. Dress in layers, with warm boots, mitts and a hat, and join the 700,000 or so residents and visitors from around the world who flock to central Ottawa-Hull each year to celebrate *Winterlude*. Thousands of celebrants of all skating abilities make the 7.8-kilometre Rideau Canal their focal point. Rent skates or a sled to pull the young ones if you need to, and use the heated shelters to warm your tingling toes during February's three-weekend Winterlude period.

Once the blades are off, many snow-loving festival goers wander over to see the exquisitely sculptured masterpieces that tower on the lawn of Parliament Hill, and at the Festival Plaza. Across from the plaza, displays of intricate, internationally carved ice sculptures grace the frozen grounds of the Crystal Garden in Confederation Park. Stop by to see this visual art soon after its completion, before Ottawa's warm winter sunshine takes its toll.

Over at Hull's Jacques Cartier Park, squeals of delight are the order of the day, as children and the young at heart streak down the giant man-made snow slides in the Snowflake Kingdom. Use the Sno-Bus shuttle to get there and to the concerts, stew cook-off and fireworks. Call 239-5000 or 1-800-465-1867, or visit www.capcan.ca.

Two other Winterlude-period events ($) prove that months of training do pay off. The *Winterlude Triathlon* (skiing, running and skating) takes place in Ottawa (call 237-7800), while in Gatineau Park, 3,000 recreational and elite participants from 20 countries challenge all or part of the *Keskinada Loppet's* trails. Races range from the 50-kilometre classic event to a two-kilometre children's race. For details call 819-595-0114, or visit www.keskinada.com.

A little further away, February's *Canadian Ski Marathon* ($) draws over 1,700 skiers to participate in all or part of a 170-kilometre race in Quebec, from Lachute to Montebello to Buckingham. Categories range from solo tourers to the coureurs de bois gold. Phone 819-770-6556, or go to www.csm-mcs.com.

Down on the St. Lawrence River, those who don't mind the cold have attended February's four-day *Gananoque Winter Festival* ($) for over 20 years. An ice-fishing derby, skating party, snowpitch tournament and torchlight parade make this a great Canadian winter celebration. From Ottawa,

Skating on the Rideau canal.

take Highway 417 West, and Highway 416 South to Kemptville. Go west on Highway 43, south again on Highway 15, and then take Highway 32. Call 382-1064.

To top off a Canadian winter in the outdoors under blue, sunny skies, the snow-laden mountains are the place to be, especially when it's festival time in one of the picturesque *Laurentian Mountain* villages. Call the tourist association (at 1-800-561-6673) for dates, and then plan a winter weekend getaway to see dogsled races, play snow ball or enjoy the ice shows and sleigh rides featured at these popular events.

DISCOVERING MORE OUTDOORS

S o far in this guide, I have described many of the interesting and exciting things I uncovered during my travels in Eastern Ontario and Western Quebec. But there's still a stack of others that I haven't mentioned yet, or that bear repeating. Included on this list are high-adrenaline activities like white-water rafting, tubing and dogsledding, as well as special places to picnic, take the kids, or go bird watching. Topics are arranged beginning with those that are really great to do soon after the melting snow is dripping from the rooftops, and budding leaves and crocuses are back on your mind.

The format is similar to that of "Outdoor Spectacles" —pick an activity and learn about some of the best places to make it happen. Again, call ahead where appropriate to confirm details before setting out, so you won't be disappointed, and count on a full-day outing in many cases, once you factor in the drive to get you there and back at a relaxed pace.

Where the Birds Are

American robin. Ring-billed gull. Canada goose. Most of us learned early to recognize the plumage colour, habitat or flight pattern of these common species. But in the case of others, such as brown-headed cowbirds, eastern meadowlarks, yellow-rumped warblers or American black ducks, for many it's an entirely different story—a bird is a bird is a bird.

However, with every passing year, more and more Canadians want to know more about the species that are regulars at their backyard feeder and those they encounter when they're out and about. As such, the number of devoted birders with their eyes trained to the sky grows every year.

For them their new hobby is easy, fun and a most enjoyable way to spend time getting closer to nature in the glorious fresh air. The National Capital Region's wide diversity of habitats and location on a migratory path provides the perfect opportunity to observe many different forest or aquatic species either close by or south along the St. Lawrence River.

To give it a try, go as you are the first time, either early in the morning or late in the evening. Move quietly and stay very still once you spot a bird. Augment your next outing with a bird identification book, a pair of binoculars (7 x 35 are recommended) and a notebook to record your discoveries. Don't forget the insect repellent!

In Ottawa, the best spot to sight forest birds flitting about is the *Britannia Conservation Area*. Songbirds, warblers, vireos and several species of waterfowl herald the return of spring as they congregate around Mud Lake, along the ridge overlooking the Ottawa River, and in the swamp, surrounded by pine and maple forests. From downtown Ottawa, travel west on Wellington Street, the Ottawa River Parkway, and Carling Avenue as far as Britannia Road. Turn right and continue to the conservation area. Park on the side streets and use the footpaths, or continue to Cassels Street and the filtration plant.

Further west along Carling Avenue, the hundreds of waterfowl resting or feeding each spring and fall at *Andrew Haydon Park's* marsh and Ottawa River beach areas paint quite a wildlife panorama. Stop by and have a look!

Because large numbers of forest birds love Ottawa's Greenbelt, American gold finches, yellow warblers, Baltimore orioles, and blue jays often skitter about among the trees along the Jack Pine Trail within the *Stony Swamp Conservation Area*. Gather a supply of sunflower seeds and the family, and from Ottawa travel east on Highway 417 to Highway 416 and then south to Hunt Club Road. Go west to Moodie Drive and left to P9.

Another time, plan to come back to enjoy the songbird's chorus along the Beaver and Chipmunk Trails. While in the area, stop at the *Wild Bird Care Centre*, where injured and orphaned species are rehabilitated and released back into the wild. The phone number is 828-2849, and to get there take the same route in the direction of the Jack Pine Trail. Exit at P8 instead, soon after you turn onto Moodie Drive.

In Ottawa's east end, *Mer Bleue* is a family bird-watching haven. Bring seeds for the chickadees that are sure to be darting about looking for a handout. From downtown Ottawa, take Highway 417 to Innes Road. Turn left and go right on Anderson Road to P19. At the boardwalk trail over the bog (further south along Anderson and then left at Ridge Road to P22) see birds more commonly found in boreal forests much further north.

Over 200 species of birds make Gatineau Park their home. To discover a peaceful and relaxing spot to study a variety of forest types, consider the trail to the *Meech Lake Ruins*. From Hull, travel north on Highway 5 and exit at Old Chelsea. Go through the village and continue on Meech Lake Road to P11 at O'Brien Beach. Take Trail 36 toward the Herridge Shelter and then go right at the signpost to the ruins.

Elsewhere in the park, turkey vultures and hawks earn many a frequent-flyer point as they glide carefree and easy through the blue summer sky at the *Champlain Lookout* along the edge of the Eardley Escarpment. Take the route described above, but turn left onto the Lake Fortune Parkway before you get to Meech Lake. At the Champlain Parkway turn right and proceed to the end.

There is no lack of places to see flocks of Canada geese stop to feed before flying south for the winter. Thousands of avid bird lovers travel to the 9,000-hectare *Upper Canada Migratory Bird Sanctuary*, on the St. Lawrence River, in late September and October. At other times of the year, four nature trails with viewing blinds conceal those combing the area looking for some of the other 150 feathered species known to hang around these parts. Think about pitching a tent on secluded Nairne Island to stay awhile ($). From Ottawa, take Highway 31 South to County Road 2 and then travel east. Call 1-800-437-2233, or visit www.parks.on.ca.

At the 264-hectare *Cooper Marsh Conservation Area*, wetland boardwalks, nature viewing/camera blinds, a tower and seven kilometres of trails allow guests the opportunity to get close to nature. Rare birds sometimes seen at this marshland and migratory-bird destination on the St. Lawrence include the black tern, the double-crested cormorant and the great egret. From Ottawa, take Highway 417 East to Highway 34. Go south to County Road 2 and then west. For information call 347-1332.

Travellers going west of Ottawa on Highway 417 and Highway 7 as far as Perth should keep an eye out for waterfowl at the *Perth Wildlife Reserve* ($ for parking), less than a kilometre south on the Rideau Ferry Road (County Road 1). Explore the nature trails winding through the property, and spend awhile in the observation tower. The phone number is 267-5721. Other great aquatic-bird-watching spots east of Ottawa are the *Casselman* (Highway 417 East) *and Embrun Lagoons* (Highway 417 East and County Road 17). These areas are extra special during migratory season.

On the Quebec side of the Ottawa River, you'll find waterfowl congregating around *Thurso* and further east at the *Plaisance Wildlife Reserve*. These marsh and field habitats make popular stopover spots during the spring and fall migration. From Hull, go east on Highway 50 and Highway 148 to the respective villages.

The last place that enters my mind when it comes to bird watching is Ottawa's *Rideau River*. Stroll its shore in search of the elegant Australian black swans and the royal swans, whose ancestors were presented to the city in 1967 by Queen Elizabeth II in honour of Canada's 100th birthday. Bring along some fresh greens from your garden (not bread), and you'll be glad you took up birding. From Ottawa, travel east on Highway 417 to Riverside Drive. Stop at the parking lot just past Billings Bridge.

For Sale Outdoors

It's a sure thing that winter boots and parkas are history for another year once the delicate spears of asparagus, early green onions and geraniums, strawflowers and impatiens are arranged picture perfectly at the outdoor market. Not many days behind, displays of plump strawberries, leafy green lettuce, seedless cucumbers, red and yellow peppers, field tomatoes, firm peaches and husks of cream corn and fragrant basil pique the senses. It's the best invitation I know to fill your picnic basket and take some of the country's crop home.

In Eastern Ontario, opportunities for market shopping abound. Some of the most popular stalls are at Ottawa's *Byward Market*, located a block east of Sussex Drive on Market Street between George and York. It's open in full force seven days a week during the growing season. Maple syrup is sold year-round, and in December Christmas trees and cedar and pine holiday decorations add to the colour of the season.

The *Parkdale Market* on Parkdale Avenue between Wellington Street and Scott Street is another Ottawa venue that has replenished kitchens for over 75 years. Primarily operating between mid May and mid November, this marketplace offers a wide array of fresh fruits and vegetables and multi-coloured annuals and perennials for sale from dawn to dusk.

South of Ottawa along the St. Lawrence River, vendors at the *Brockville Farmer's Market* (open Tuesday, Thursday and Saturday), and the *Gananoque Farmer's Market* (open Saturday mornings only) sell farm produce, delicious apple pies and cakes and handicrafts of all sorts.

A little farther west, Tuesday, Thursday and Saturday are the days to visit the *Kingston Farmer's Market*. Open all year, this outdoor market, located behind city hall, a block or so from Lake Ontario, operates from 6:00 A.M. to 6:00 P.M.

For many throughout the Ottawa Valley, a trip to a country market has become a memorable Saturday-morning shopping ritual. As the seasons progress, the bounty of fruits and vegetables harvested changes as well. Stop by often at any of these spots close to Ottawa-Hull to fill your pantry, freezer or storage cellar for the cold winter ahead. Use a highway map to locate the town and follow the signs or the locals once you're there.

At the *Metcalfe Farmer's Market*, southeast of Ottawa, locally produced agricultural products and delicious home-baked pies and cinnamon buns are for sale at the fairgrounds from late May to mid October. If travelling west

Byward Market

of the city, consider a stop at either the *Carp, Renfrew or Cobden Farmer's Markets,* or at the one a bit farther away at *Perth*.

To shop outdoors for items other than fruit and vegetables, visit the famous *Stittsville Flea Market,* west of Ottawa off Highway 417 at Exit 144 (County Road 5). Here, CDs, clothes, furniture, and blankets share space with crafts and an eclectic array of odds and ends that appeal to Sunday bargain hunters all year long.

Back in Ottawa, very special finds can be made at the *Great Glebe Garage Sale,* held annually on the last Saturday of May. Smart shoppers arrive early to stroll this upscale neighbourhood in search of designer and antique items of all shapes and sizes. From downtown Ottawa, travel on Mackenzie Avenue and then Wellington Street to Bank Street. Go left to find a garage-sale-lovers paradise between Highway 417 and Holmwood. Call 564-1058 for information.

Let's Go for a Picnic

Imagine laying out a spread fit for the queen in a picturesque setting on a warm summer day. Perhaps your wicker basket is packed with something simple like cheese, crackers, fruit and fancy napkins, or instead you've prepared a truly gourmet feast to savour in the glorious fresh air with a special friend or the whole family.

Whatever your plans, remember that perishable foods such as salads, meats and dairy products must be kept cold. A cooler chest and inexpensive re-freezable cold packs or frozen personal-size fruit-juice boxes should do the trick. Try adding a shot of lemon juice to water before freezing to make it taste better once it warms.

Picnic season is short, so keep easy meal fixings, plates, utensils, red and white checked tablecloths, napkins, hand wipes, insect repellent, easy-fold chairs or a blanket handy at all times so you can act on impulse and pack up in a jiffy. If you're not in the mood to make your lunch or dinner, pick up something special along the way.

Outdoor meal opportunities abound along any of the cycling, hiking, cross-country skiing or autoroutes previously discussed. Included here are spots in the Ottawa-Hull area that deserve special mention.

In you're out and about exploring downtown Ottawa and you feel like an impromptu meal, there are a few places to enjoy lunch outdoors. Pick up some fresh goodies in the Byward Market and head a short distance to one of the premiere picnic spots in the whole of Canada. Find a table at the north end of *Major's Hill Park*, not far from the statue of the Anishinabe Scout, and marvel at the million-dollar view of historic Ottawa. The magnificent Parliamentary Library and Peace Tower are in front of you, so don't forget your camera.

An equally impressive spot is found a short walk up the hill beside the National Gallery. From *Nepean Point*, a statue of Samuel de Champlain surveys the river he travelled up in 1613. You'll have a chance to do the same once you've spread your food out on the bleachers of the Astrolabe theatre.

If you're anxious to eat soon after you've picked up designer pizza or shwarmas in the Byward Market, some delightful squares less than half a block from Sussex Drive make perfect quick-stop, park-bench picnic stops. The first European-style *courtyard* is tucked away discretely behind the stone buildings on George Street. The birds and squirrels have already found it, so be willing to share.

Alternatively, a half block away, rest a bit in the company of a smiling dancing bear while enjoying an outdoor lunch in *Jeanne d' Arc Court* (between York and Clarence) or continue straight ahead to a bench near the *Tin House* sculpture and the splashing fountain (between Clarence Street and Murray Street).

To work up an appetite, buy some food in the Byward Market and then hike across the Alexandra Bridge to the grounds of Hull's *Canadian Museum of Civilization*. Pick a spot along the shore of the Ottawa River to enjoy a postcard-perfect view of Parliament Hill, the Ottawa locks, Supreme Court and National Library as you munch lunch on a park bench or on the lawn.

Further away, *Maple or Green Island*, in the Rideau River, provides an idyllic backdrop for a romantic meal spread out on the manicured lawns near the slow-moving water. To get there from downtown Ottawa, take Sussex Drive to Stanley Avenue. Park close to the Minto Bridges and walk a short distance to choose a spot close by, or go a bit further to locate one behind the former Ottawa City Hall.

Those picnicking at *Rockcliffe Park* will be welcomed by panoramic vistas of the Ottawa and Gatineau Rivers, in a beautiful setting complete with gigantic trees. Picnic tables accommodate groups, and if it rains there's a pavilion to nip into. To get there take Sussex Drive as well. After the road becomes the Rockcliffe Parkway, look for the park's entrance on the left.

Another time, travel from downtown on the Queen Elizabeth Driveway and Prince of Wales Drive to the *Dominion Arboretum*, with its 30 hectares boasting 2,400 different varieties and species of trees and shrubs. Take a stroll later to see the Rideau Canal and Dows Lake, and the ornamental gardens at the Central Experimental Farm.

Further along Prince of Wales Drive are two other favourite outdoor meal-time haunts. Go left on Heron Road to the first at *Vincent Massey Park*, a 28.9-hectare green oasis that is perfect for individual or group picnics. Bring a ball or the lawn darts to wile away a sunny summer Sunday. To find *Hog's Back Park*, turn left off Prince of Wales instead, onto Hog's Back Road. While you're there, take time to have a look at the thundering waterfalls smack in the heart of Ottawa.

In the western part of the city, *Andrew Haydon Park* has plenty of space as well for outdoor mealtime entertaining. Kids will love it here, because as a prelude to dinner they can have fun at the water play structure next door. Later, go back down the path a short stretch and choose a picnic table near a barbecue. From downtown Ottawa, travel on Mackenzie Avenue, left on Wellington Street, and Carling Avenue to Acres Road. Call 820-1486.

Further west, the new picnic area at *Shirleys Bay*, in the Greenbelt, provides pleasing views of the Ottawa River, Gatineau Hills and the waterfowl that call this place home. From Ottawa, travel west on Highway 417 and north on Moodie Drive to Carling Avenue. Go left here and then right on Range Road to P1.

Each picnic season, a meal in magnificent Gatineau Park is essential on a warm summer day. The *Étienne-Brûlé Lookout* is a favourite of many, with the Ottawa River Valley and the lush green fields of the Pontiac region unfolded at your feet. From downtown Hull, take Laurier Street and Alexandre-Taché Boulevard to the Gatineau Park Entrance. Follow the Gatineau Parkway, and turn left onto the Champlain Parkway and watch for the signs.

A second inviting spot in the park is the *Old Chelsea Picnic Field*. From Hull, travel north on Highway 5 to Exit 12 for Old Chelsea. Turn left and into the village, where you can pick up some delicious sandwiches, squares or cookies at the wonderful bakery before turning left onto Kingsmere Road and going a short distance. After you've eaten, go down the stairs to have a look at rushing Chelsea Creek and then take the path up to the left to find the Protestant burial grounds where Asa Meech (of Meech Lake) and Thomas Wright, the brother of Philomen Wright who founded Hull, are buried.

Excursions for Kids—Young and Old

You don't need children or even grandchildren for that matter to enjoy these made-for-kids places that are guaranteed to make you feel young again.

In Ottawa, a favourite year-round outing for kids from 1 to 91 is a trip to the *Central Experimental Farm* ($) to see the pigs, sheep, goats, rabbits and poultry. Visit the dairy herd to pet their faces or come later in the afternoon to see them milked. Stop to see Roseanne, who survived the devastating fire of 1996, or enjoy a ride on the Tally-Ho Wagon. From downtown Ottawa, travel along the Queen Elizabeth Driveway and Prince of Wales Drive to the traffic circle, then go right. For information, call 991-3044, or visit www.agriculture.nmstc.ca.

Another time, take the children along to feed the sheep and goats at the *Valleyview Little Animal Farm* ($). Later, stroll over to view the ponies, horses, llamas and emus, before boarding the train for a ride through crops of corn, wheat, pumpkins and sunflowers. Pack along a lunch. From Ottawa, travel west on Highway 417 and take Highway 416 as far as Exit 66 at Fallowfield Road. Go right at the end of the ramp and one kilometre to number 4750. Call 591-1126, or go to www.vvlittleanimalfarm.com.

A different kind of spot that the kids will enjoy on a warm, summery weekend afternoon is *Pinhey's Point*. Located on a secluded bay of the Ottawa River, with the Gatineau Hills as a serene backdrop, kids love touring the historic Pinhey home ($), splashing about in the water and participating in the exciting theme events. Travel west on Highway 417 and take the March Road Exit. Proceed north to Dunrobin Road, then right on Riddell Road, which becomes 6th Line. Watch for the signs. For more information call 832-4347, or visit www.city.kanata.on.ca.

Also west of the city, children of all ages are likely to give a five-star rating to the special happenings throughout the year at the *Saunders Farm* ($) in Munster. For example, each October the barn of terror, haunted hayride and amazing mazes make the farm the eeriest place in these parts. Take Highway 417 West and then Exit 138 (Eagleson Road). Go left, continue to Fallowfield Road, turn right and travel to Munster Road. Turn left, continue to Bleeks Road and turn right to the farm at number 7893. Phone 838-5440, or go to the website at www.saundersfarm.com.

The Central Experimental Farm

Children young and old all remember a favourite bedtime story, and *Storyland* ($) welcomes the whole family to meander through its 33-acre forest in search of Cinderella, Red Riding Hood, Alice in Wonderland and the Mad Hatter. The kids may even get a chance to attend a puppet show, shake hands with some nursery characters or cool off at the Splish/Splash Water Spray Park on a hot day. Travel west on Highway 417 and Highway 17 and turn right on Storyland Road (County Road 4). For details call 432-2222 or 1-800-205-3695, or go to www.storyland.on.ca.

East of Ottawa-Hull, the *Papanack Park Zoo* ($) offers a great spot for youngsters to observe tigers, bears, wolves, white lion cubs and a whole host of barnyard animals up close. Take Highway 417 East and Highway 174 to Wendover. Turn right on County Road 19 (Nine Mile Road), and travel about a kilometre. Call 673-7275, or visit www.papanack.com.

Out that way as well, cast a line at the *Outaouais Fish Farm* ($) and make the first catch of the season. Trout fishing is available without a licence in the two stocked ponds. Travel east on Highway 417 and Highway 174 past Rockland. Turn right on Landry Road (County Road 8) and then left on Clark Road so the kids can try their luck. Call 446-5057, or go to www.cyberus.ca/~pisc.gl.

At the *Cumberland Heritage Village Museum* ($), take a peek at how things used to be back in the good ol' days. At the former Vars railway station, get a map showing where to find the sawmill, hay barn, church and one-room school, which are some of the many buildings that have been moved to this site from various neighbouring communities. Take Highway 417 and Highway 174 East to Cumberland and follow the signs to 2940 Queen Street. For more information call 833-3059.

A larger place, similar in concept, is *Upper Canada Village* ($) on the St. Lawrence River. Plan to spend a whole day at this spot (named the 1999 Best National Attraction), exploring fully functional mills, heritage homes, trade shops, churches and farms that date back to the 1860s. Costumed interpreters and farm animals help bring the village to life. From Ottawa, take Highway 31 (Bank Street) South to Highway 401. Go east towards Cornwall and exit at Upper Canada Road (Exit 758). Go south to County Road 2 and left to the village. You can reach the village at 543-3704 or 1-800-437-2233, or see the website at www.uppercanadavillage.com.

Dinosaurs are all the craze these days, so after visiting Upper Canada Village, it's worthwhile to stop at *Prehistoric World* ($) nearby to see whether you'll recognize the brontosaurus, stegosaurus, tyrannosaurus rex or triceratops among the 51 full-sized exhibits. Call 543-2503.

On the Quebec side of the Ottawa River, there's nowhere in the world water-loving kids would rather be on a hot summer day than riding a raft down the twisting Mammoth River Ride or challenging the Kamikaze at the

Mont Cascades Waterpark ($). Take Highway 50 East from Hull to the Archambault Boulevard Exit. Turn right onto Highway 307 and continue north to Cantley. At the bottom of the hill, turn left onto Mont Cascades Road. Phone 819-827-0301 or 1-888-282-2722, or visit www.montcascades.ca.

Continue further east on Highway 50 and Highway 148 and left on Highway 323 to *Parc Omega* ($). Here, from the safety of their vehicle, children will have the opportunity to view animals such as bison and moose living in the wild. There may even be a chance to feed a few of the creatures that live in this wilderness park. Phone 819-423-5487, or go to www.parc-omega.com.

As the climax to a year of kid-type explorations, dress the whole family warmly for a stroll around Parliament Hill and Confederation Boulevard each December. That's when *Christmas Lights Across Canada* lights up Ottawa's heart in a magical display of colour. Make sure to walk behind the Centre Block to see the trees lit up across the river, and then take a trip up the Peace Tower to view the spectacle from above. While you're inside, make a wish beside one of the tallest decorated Christmas trees in Canada. Call 239-5000 or 1-800-465-1867, or visit www.capcan.ca.

Horseback Riding

Take one horse and rider and add blue sky and miles of breathtaking coun-tryside, and you have the perfect recipe for a heavenly day. The Ottawa-Hull area is blessed with all the ingredients for the mix—wonderful trails that travel peaceful back-country roads, or those that cut through tall, restful forests and fields of sweet-smelling grasses and colourful flowers. To sample the finished product yourself, why not don your jeans and shoes with a heel, and climb into the saddle to enjoy a special back-to-nature experience.

If you don't have your own animal, all of the area's trail-riding stables provide horses ($) ranging from those that are ideal for the first-time rider right up to ones that the experienced horse person will enjoy. Call ahead to confirm the length of ride you are interested in before heading out.

About 20 minutes east of Ottawa, the *Happy Trails Riding Stables* has provided western trail rides through the lush countryside for almost 25 years. Haunted hayrides are a favourite with the younger set at Halloween, and the office gang loves the wintertime sleigh rides. From Ottawa, take Highway 417 East to the Anderson Road Exit. Go left and then right onto Russell Road. Continue and take the fork to Leitrim Road. Go to the end. For more information about the stable call 822-1482, or visit their website at www.ottawa.com/happytrails.

If the kids are into pony or horseback riding, the *Pinto Valley Ranch* has offered rides by the hour for over forty years. From Ottawa, travel west on

Highway 417 and take March Road North. Turn right at Dunrobin Road and continue for about 30 minutes to Galetta Road. Turn here and keep going to number 1969. The phone number is 623-3439, and the web address www.pintovalley.com.

On the Quebec side of the Ottawa River, west of Hull, the family can enjoy a day of horseback riding in Gatineau Park, or a hay or sleigh ride with a whole gang at the *Luskville Falls Ranch*. From downtown Hull, take Hwy 148 West (drive left along Laurier Street, Alexandre-Taché Boulevard and Aylmer Road. Turn right at Park Street and then onto Eardley Road) and proceed as far as Luskville. Continue past the town hall and watch for the signs. Phone 819-455-2290.

Another favourite Quebec horse-lovers spot is *Captiva Farms*. Explore 40 kilometres of the scenic Gatineau hills and stay over if you wish along the way at one of the lakes that dot the landscape. Travel north on Highway 5 and 105 past Wakefield. Go east on Highway 366 over the Gatineau River and then continue to Chemin de la Montagne and turn left. Call 819-459-2769, or visit www3.sympatico.ca/horseback.riding.

White-Water Rafting

Annually, thrill seekers from the area and around the globe shoot the world-class rapids of the Ottawa and Rouge Rivers. On the international scale, the most turbulent of the waters rate up to 5.5 out of 6 in the early spring when the flow is high and rushing fast. As summer approaches, a score of 3 or 4 still makes the raging river's foam challenging.

On these waterways, rafting trips ($) for individuals or for the whole family range from half-day excursions to those that last several days. All equipment, including wetsuits, is either supplied or available for rent, and tasty meals barbecued at a stop along the way beside a crackling bonfire enhance the rafting experience. In some cases, kayaking and camping is also possible. Reservations and precise directions as to the start/pick-up location and clothing required are necessary before heading out.

The Ottawa River's two channels, the Main and the Middle, make for great thrill-of-a lifetime rafting experiences, especially from mid June onward, when the water has lost its icy winter chill. Names like Angel's Kiss, Butcher's Knife and the Coliseum give you a hint of what you're in for.

To give it a try, call any of these Ontario companies to arrange an excursion through very spectacular scenery, about an hour and a half or so west of Ottawa-Hull. *Wilderness Tours* can be reached at 1-800-267-9166 or www.wildernesstours.com, *OWL Rafting* at 1-800-461-7238 or www.owl-mkc.ca, and *River Run* at 1-800-267-8504 or www.riverrunners.com.

Equally exhilarating outings can be arranged on the Quebec side of the Ottawa River through *Esprit Rafting*, at 1-800–596-7238 or www.espritrafting.com; *Ottawa Adventures Rafting*, at 1–800–690-7238 or www.ottawaadventures.qc.ca; or at *Equinox Adventures*, at 1-800–785-8855 or www.equinoxadventures.com.

In Quebec, an hour or so east of Ottawa-Hull, try *New World*, at 1-800-361-5033 or www.newworld.ca, or *Aventures en EauVive* at 1-800-567-6881 or www.aventureseneauvive.qc.ca to arrange a boredom-busting kind of day tackling the wild waters of the Rouge River.

Canoeing

When I laid eyes on my first voyageur canoe, I was immediately taken back to the days when I studied Canadian history in elementary school. I still remember hearing about explorers like Anthony Henday, Peter Pond and David Thompson, and can envision their travels in birch-bark canoes past waterfalls, around rapids and through the spectacular scenery of Alberta and Saskatchewan.

Before the prairies opened up, Native Canadians and explorers had been paddling up and down the Ottawa River's major trade route for years. To get a feel for their nautical experience, reserve a time to take the whole family canoeing in the Ottawa-Hull area.

From the *Canadian Museum of Civilization* ($) in Hull, a guide will join you in a voyageur canoe as you glide along the Ottawa River for a couple of hours, enjoying a close-up look at the Ottawa Locks, the Parliament Buildings and the extraordinary landscape that makes Canada's capital so unique. For details phone 819-827-4467, or go to www.orbit.qc.ca/canoe.

For a one-to-three-day paddling excursion on the famous Rocher-Fendu section of the Ottawa River, climb aboard an eight-metre voyageur canoe with *Canadian Voyageur Adventures* ($), and travel along this mighty waterway with an authentically dressed guide. Stop part way along to enjoy the kind of foods eaten by the early adventurers. Call 1-800-833-5055 or visit www.gocanoe.com.

In Luskville, a historic outing for six or more adults can be arranged with *Au Charme de la Montagne* ($) along part of the route travelled by the Hudson's Bay fur traders as they transported their precious cargo. A highlight is seeing some of the old portage spots. Call 819-455-9158.

At Merrickville's *Ron Johnstone Paddling Centre* ($), south of Ottawa on the Rideau River, outdoor enthusiasts can rent a voyageur canoe for the day or a few hours through the Canadian Recreational Canoeing Association. Groups of 20 or more can sign up for an interpretive program to learn more about the early explorers and fur traders while their large vessel glides through the water. Call 269-2910 or 1-888-252-6292.

In Eastern Ontario and Western Quebec there are also lots of picturesque waterways waiting to be navigated by "ordinary" canoe. The Rideau Canal,

Canoeing through the locks on the Rideau Canal.

Frontenac Provincial Park and the St. Lawrence Seaway, around the Thousand Islands, are all sure to be on the list. An excellent map of routes throughout Eastern Canada can be obtained through the Ontario East Tourism Association ($), at 1-800-567-3278 or www.ontarioeast.com.

In Gatineau Park, Meech, Philippe and La Pêche Lakes are favourite spots for canoeing and/or canoe-camping in *Gatineau Park*. Call 819-827-2020.

Further from Ottawa-Hull, canoe at the *Papineau-Labelle Wildlife Reserve*, which may be reached at 1-800-665-6527, or in *Mont Tremblant Park*, at 819-688-2281. At many of these locations, canoes are available for rent so that you can enjoy a lazy summer afternoon with only the dipping of your paddles to disturb your thoughts.

Another option is to rent a canoe and be shuttled to a drop-off spot for a day of relaxation. Think about trying this along the Quebec's scenic Gatineau River or at the lakes hidden away in the Gatineau Hills, with either *Expedition Radisson* ($) in Wakefield, at 819-459-3860 or 1–888–459-3860, or *Paugan Falls Canoe Works* ($) in Low, at 819-422-3456 or www.magma.ca\~paufacan. Inquire about a trip to Lac St. Marie or to Green Lake, a secret wilderness paradise that lives up to its name.

Scuba Diving

Who would ever believe that we have some of the best freshwater diving in the world right here in Eastern Ontario? Scattered along the floor of the *St. Lawrence River* between Brockville and Kingston are the remains of steamers, schooners and car ferries. Some of these ships date back as far as the War of 1812.

This navigational graveyard is a diver's paradise, as the cargo holds, masts, booms and wheelhouses are well preserved and the water is relatively warm. With visibility up to 24 metres in spots, one can sometimes spot sunfish, bass, carp or muskie cruising around this place they call home.

Beginners can sign up for lessons to become certified in this adventure sport, before heading off for an unforgettable day or weekend-long underwater experience to see the Rothesay, the Kingshorn or the Wolfe Islander II. Experienced divers can join the thousands who come this way to go shipwreck exploring annually, off chartered boats or the shore.

A few of the diving operations in the area that rent gear, provide certified guides and make tour arrangements ($) include *Burton's Dive Service* at 745-6444, or www.burtonsdive.com; *Country Divers*, at 798–1867; *Kingston Diving Centre*, at 634-8464 or *Sea n' Sky Scuba* at 925-0308.

Be sure to inquire about lessons if diving is new to you. Become an experienced scuba diver in Ontario so you can enhance your next vacation in the Florida Keys or Australia's Great Barrier Reef.

Tobogganing and Tubing

Down, down, down. Tossing and turning on the hard-packed snow. Tobogganing and tubing enthusiasts love it, and there's no shortage of great spots in and around Ottawa-Hull where for the whole family can participate.

Before heading out, make sure to pack layers of warm clothing, a safety helmet and ski goggles or a balaclava to protect your face as you pick up speed. Whatever you do, forget about the scarves, as these could prove dangerous if they get caught up in this or that when you're on the slopes.

In and around Ottawa, there are a few choices when it comes to streaking down the hill. For those wishing to be whisked up the hill by automated lift rather than hiking to the top themselves, several privately operated hills supply both the tubes and the transportation.

Both *Vorlage* ($) and *Mount Pakenham* ($) maintain snow-tubing lanes and automatic lifts as part of their downhill-ski operation. To locate Vorlage from Hull, take Highway 5 and Highway 105 North and proceed into Wakefield. Turn left on Burnside Road. Vorlage may be reached at 819-459-2301 or 1–877-867-5243, or by visiting www.skivorlage.com. Get to Mount Pakenham by going west from Ottawa on Highway 417 and Highway 17 to Arnprior. Turn left at Antrim onto County Road 20 and follow the signs. Call 624-5290 or 1-800-665-7105 or check out www.mountpakenham.com.

Le Domaine ($), in Quebec, also employs lifts to take sliding enthusiasts back up the slope on multi-coloured tubes. From Hull, travel east on Highway 50 to Masson. Exit at Laurentides Avenue, turn left at the stop sign and follow the signs. Phone 819-281-0299.

If, on the other hand, you prefer riding their your own toboggan or inner tube and hauling it back up the hill on shank's mare, grab yours and head for the hills. The *Greens Creek Conservation Area* hill in Ottawa's Greenbelt is popular because it offers a variety of terrain and is lit in the evening. From Ottawa, take Highway 417 and Highway 174 East to the Montreal Road Exit. Go east on St. Joseph Boulevard and turn right at Bearbrook Road to P24.

Kids of all ages on crazy carpets love the *Conroy Pit* slope. To get there from Ottawa, take Highway 417 East and turn onto Walkley Road. Proceed straight, turn left on Conroy, and continue south past Hunt Club Road about two kilometres to P15 and to the hill, which is lit until 11:00 P.M.

The younger set may enjoy the third Greenbelt toboggan run the best of all, as the hill is not too steep or bumpy. But sliding is only possible during daylight at *Bruce Pit*. From Ottawa, take Highway 417 West and exit left at Highway 416. Continue south to the Hunt Club Road Exit. Turn left (east) onto Hunt Club, going back over the Highway 416 overpass. Go left at Cedarview Road and proceed to P12.

Some of the steepest toboggan hills around Ottawa-Hull are at the Central Experimental Farm's *Arboretum*. The two slopes—one towards Dows Lake, the other towards the Rideau Canal—are reached from downtown Ottawa by taking Mackenzie Avenue and Colonel By Drive to the Pretoria Bridge. Go right here and then left onto Queen Elizabeth Drive which later becomes Prince of Wales Drive. Turn left at the traffic circle at the top of the hill.

Another spot thrill seekers head for is the hill at *Mooney's Bay*. From downtown Ottawa, go south on Mackenzie Avenue and Colonel By Drive to Hog's Back Road. Turn left here and proceed to the parking lot on your left.

If height is what you're looking for when you're challenging the slopes, travel west on Highway 417 to the Carling Avenue Exit. Proceed west to Clyde Avenue and turn left to find the old ski hill at *Carlington Park*. In what used to be the city of Kanata, about twenty minutes further west, the man-made, 12-metre-high hill at *Walter Baker Park*, off Terry Fox Drive, is very fast and rough.

Hang on!

Downhill Skiing

The magic of a Canadian winter is too special to be spent indoors staring at the tube or the computer screen. Blue sky, cherry-red cheeks, tingling toes and cups of whipped-cream-topped hot chocolate are all part of the cold-weather game, that make for long-to-be-talked-about moments in the great outdoors.

The perfect way to enhance November-to-March memories is to spend a few days on the slopes. If you know how to downhill ski or snowboard, you're all set to take advantage of the many opportunities in Eastern Ontario and Western Quebec, where you can soak up some sunshine and crisp, fresh air while swooshing down the hill. If you need to learn how to participate in these sports, all ski resorts in the area have rental shops and offer private or group lessons ($) to get you started.

For some, people watching seems preferable to snowplowing when it comes to being outdoors in the cold. That's fine. Pick a glorious winter day and relax on of one of the après-ski chalet's decks, tracking skiers streaking down the hill in a blazing fashion show of colour. Next time, plan to join in.

Whichever option you're up for, several busy spots within an hour and a half of Ottawa-Hull provide slopes for all skiing abilities and a place to enjoy a delicious lunch or snack. Purchase an hourly, daily, evening or season's pass ($) depending on how long you plan to ski and the location selected.

On the Quebec side of the Ottawa River, the closest ski hill to Ottawa-Hull is Gatineau Park's *Camp Fortune*, with a vertical height of 213 metres. Great views, 20 alpine runs, a snowboard park and 7 lifts await enthusiastic beginners and experts from mid November to late April. Evening skiing is also sometimes available. From Hull, take Highway 5 North to Exit 12 for Old Chelsea. Turn left and continue through the village and onto Meech Lake Road. Watch for the signs. Camp Fortune may be reached at 819-827-1717 or 1-888-283-1717, or by going to www.campfortune.com.

Mont Cascades, a year-round playground in the Outaouais, offers day and evening skiers or snowboarders the challenge of a 160-metre vertical drop, 30 minutes or so from Parliament Hill. There are 14 runs, 4 chairlifts and 2 t-bars to keep visitors moving. From Hull, take Highway 50 East. Exit at Archambault Boulevard, turn right onto Highway 307 and continue north to Cantley. At the bottom of the hill, turn left onto Mont Cascades Road. For more information call 819-827-0301 or 1-888-282-2722, or visit www.montcascades.ca.

Vorlage specializes in family wintertime fun. Located in the village of Wakefield, this 50-year-old resort has 15 trails (12 of them lit at night) and a total of 5 lifts and t-bars to get skiers up the 152 vertical metres. The tops of the slopes afford panoramic views of the Gatineau River. There's also a snow-tubing park and skating rink for the non-skiing crowd. From Hull, take Highway 5 and Highway 105 North to Wakefield. In the village, turn left at Burnside Road. Phone 819-459-2301 or 1-877-867-5243, or go to www.skivorlage.com.

Edelweiss, a short distance from Wakefield, is a 40-year-old, family-owned ski and snowboard resort. The Edelweiss Mountain has 4 chair lifts and 200 metres of vertical rise, to suit abilities from beginner to expert on 18 runs (14 are lit at night). From Hull, take Highway 5 and Highway 105 North to Wakefield. Travel east on Highway 366 to the resort. For details call 819-459-2328 or check out www.edelweissvalley.com.

Mont St. Marie, the première ski resort in the Outaouais, has a 381-metre vertical drop. Twenty-four trails on two mountains challenge all levels of skiers. For those who prefer snowboarding, there's a permanent cross track and a competition half-pipe. Two high-speed quad lifts take skiers to the summit and a powerful snowmaking system covers 95 percent of the skiable area with the white stuff. World-Cup-style moguls add excitement. Take Highway 5 and Highway 105 North to Lac St Marie and the resort, located about 90 kilometres from Hull. Call 819-467-5200 or 1-800-567-1256, or visit the website at www.montstemarie.com.

On the Ontario side of the Ottawa River, two resorts are popular with the Ottawa area's ski set. *Mount Pakenham*, about an hour from downtown Ottawa, has 20 kilometres of cross-country trails groomed for classic or skate skiing. Alpine thrill-seekers can try 9 runs, the snowboard park or the snow-tubing hill that whisks tubers back to the top by lift. Night skiing is also possible at certain times. From Ottawa, take Highway 417 and

Highway 17 West. Turn left at Antrim onto County Road 20 and follow the signs. The phone number is 624-5290 or 1-800-665-7105 or check out www.mountpakenham.com.

Calabogie Peaks, a four-season resort about an hour and a half west of Ottawa-Hull, has a 231-metre vertical drop, 22 downhill runs and a snowboarding park. Opportunities for cross-country skiing and snowshoeing are nearby. From Ottawa, take Highway 417 and Highway 17 West past Arnprior. About ten kilometres further, turn left onto Calabogie Road and proceed to the southwest shore of the lake. Call 752-2720 or 1-800-669-4861, or go to www.calabogie.com.

If you feel up to driving to the Laurentians, about two to three hours from Ottawa-Hull, on roads that are generally well-maintained in the winter, a European-style skiing experience awaits, without the hassles of exchanging currency, overcoming jet lag or understanding a foreign language. Located north of the St. Lawrence River in southwestern Quebec, the highest peak is 1,190 metres.

When the weather is warm, thousands come to this area to get up close and personal with nature, but it's the downhill skiing and snowboarding slopes that keep them coming back. There are several fabulous mountain areas to choose from, each with its own personality. To take a mini vacation when you're there, call the Laurentian Tourist Association for accommodation ideas, at 1-800-561-6673, or visit their website at www.laurentides.com.

Mont Tremblant or the "trembling mountain" is by far the most famous ski resort in the Laurentians. This impressive North American ski destination has attracted millions of ski enthusiasts from around the world over its 60-year history. Ninety-two runs offer downhill terrain for all levels, while twelve lifts whisk skiers to the top of the mountain, with its vertical drop of 650 metres. State-of-the-art snowmaking equipment keeps the slopes snow covered from December to late April, to the delight of those who enjoy skiing by day and life in the slope-side village after hours. Mont Tremblant also specializes in snowboarding slopes for those who prefer to challenge the mountain this way, and skating, snowshoeing and dogsledding for those not into heights. From Hull, take Highway 50 and Highway 148 East to Montebello. Take Highway 323 North to St-Jovite and go left on Highway 117 North and past the village about two kilometres to Montée Ryan. Turn right at the traffic light and follow the signs. You can call 1-888-736-2526, or visit www.tremblant.ca.

Enjoy Quebec's traditional joie de vivre at the *Gray Rocks* all-season playground just south of Mont Tremblant. With a vertical drop of 191 metres, its 24 slopes and 4 lifts provide local and international guests with great skiing, snowboarding and snowblading. Pioneers of the all-inclusive ski week, Gray Rocks continues to remain a top-notch spot for those wanting to learn about alpine skiing or to sharpen their skills. Cross-country skiing on 100 kilometres of groomed trails in the Mont Tremblant/St-Jovite area, snowmobiling and snowshoeing add to the resort's popularity. From Hull, follow the directions to Mont Tremblant as far as Montée Ryan. Continue on this road and then turn right on Highway 327 South. For information call 819-425-2771 or 1-800-567-6767, or visit www.grayrocks.com.

Mont Blanc continues to challenge skiers and snowboarders annually on 36 runs down the second-highest peak in the Laurentians. About 40 percent of the trails are rated difficult over the three mountain faces, with a vertical elevation of 300 metres and 7 lifts taking skiers to the top. From Hull, follow the directions to St-Jovite and then take Highway 117 South to St-Faustin-Lac-Carré. Call 819-688-2444 or 1-800-567–6715, or go to the website at www.ski-mont-blanc.com.

Each winter, the St-Saveur Valley draws thousands to the largest night-skiing area in the world. Skiers keep coming back to experience *Mont St-Saveur's* 213-metre vertical drop and 29 slopes, 24 of which are lit at night. As well, 24 kilometres of cross-country trails and après-ski fun in the one-hundred-year-old village at its base make this a great place to enjoy winter. Affiliated spots nearby, including *Mont Avila, Mont Gabriel* and *Mont Olympia* and *Morin Heights,* all have perfect slopes for family fun. From Hull, take Highway 50, Highway 148 and Highway 158 East to Highway 15. Turn north and find Exit 58 or 60. Phone 1-800-363-2426, or visit www.montsaintsaveur.com.

Ste-Adèle's Chantecler 200-metre vertical drop is the final Laurentian spot where you can barrel down the hill on skis. Night skiing on over half of the resort's 23 slopes, cross-country skiing on well-groomed trails and the charming resort village are all star attractions. Follow the directions above to Highway 15. Go north to Exit 67. Call 450-229-3555 or 1-800-363-2420.

Note: When romancing the Laurentians, travel the same route as the "snow trains" did in the 1920s. From early December until mid April, between St-Jérôme and Val-David, you can glide along groomed cross-country trails. During the same period, snowmobile enthusiasts have the P'tit Train du Nord Linear Park to themselves, between Ste-Agathe-Sud and Mont-Laurier. Stops at any of the charming villages, or a rest in the restored railway stations add enjoyment to any outdoor winter adventure. Refer to a P'tit Train du Nord Linear Park map to help decide where to begin an outing, or call the tourist association for suggestions.

Dogsledding

To experience a taste of what life is like in Canada's north, head out on an adventure by sled in Western Quebec. Hold on tight as teams of Siberian Huskies, Malamutes or Malamute crosses whisk you off across the serene winter countryside. Sled dogs pride themselves in taking a sled from a standstill to 60 or 70 kilometres per hour in no time flat when the weather is cold and crisp and the snow deep. You're in for a thrill!

At *Expedition Radisson*, enroll in Dogsledding 101 to learn how to stand on the sled's runners and the lingo to make the team stop and move forward, before heading out on an excursion lasting a few hours or several days. From Hull, travel north on Highway 5 and Highway 105 to Wakefield. The phone number is 819-459-3860 or 1-888-459-3860.

About an hour and a quarter from Ottawa-Hull, you can explore the Petite-Nation back country by driving your own dog team or relying on an experienced musher to navigate. Exhilarating trips for an hour or a day over 40 kilometres of trails can be arranged at *Les Randonnées Chez Marcel.* From Hull, travel east on Highway 50 and Highway 148 to Papineauville. From here it's 20–25 minutes north on Highway 321. Call 819-983-2986.

The last great spot where you can do some mushing not far from Canada's capital is at the *Devine Resort*. Plan to stay over so you can add some cross-country ski time to a winter getaway. From Ottawa, travel east on Highway 417, go north at Exit 88 and then a short distance to Devine Road. Turn right here and proceed to number 3948. Phone 835-4095 or 1–888-379-9687, or go to www.aventure-canadienne.com.

Index